The Stage Directions Guide to Auditions

The Stage Directions Guide to Auditions

Edited by
Stephen Peithman
Neil Offen

HEINEMANN
Portsmouth, NH

HEINEMANN
A division of Reed Elsevier Inc.
361 Hanover Street
Portsmouth, NH 03801–3912
http://www.heinemann.com

Offices and agents throughout the world

The editors and publisher wish to thank those who have generously given permission to reprint borrowed material:
"Improving Your Audition Technique" by David Pogue originally appeared as "Escape from Audition Hell" in *The MTI Times Newsletter* (Fall 1995). Reprinted with permission of the publisher.
"Children Will Listen" by Lee Morgan was originally published in *Spotlight* (May/June 1995). Reprinted by permission of The Little Theatre of Winston-Salem.

LIBRARY OF CONGRESS CATALOGING-IN-PUBLICATION DATA
Peithman, Stephen.
    The stage directions guide to auditions / Stephen Peithman and Neil Offen.
        p. cm.
    ISBN 0-325-00083-2
        1. Acting—Auditions. I. Offen, Neil. II. Title.
    PN2071.A92P45 1998
    792'.028—dc21   98-28883
                                                                                          CIP

Editor: Lisa A. Barnett
Production: Abigail M. Heim
Cover design: Barbara Werden
Cover photo: Rob Karosis
Manufacturing: Louise Richardson

Printed in the United States of America on acid-free paper

02 01 00 99 98 DA 1 2 3 4 5

For all those in front of the lights and behind the scenes
who understand the magic of theatre

Contents

Foreword

*S*omething new and different, *The Stage Directions Guide to Auditions* is the first look at the audition process from the perspective of both actor and director.

Both parties know that auditions are often stressful since in a short time directors must make judgments on actors' ability to serve the needs of the production, while actors must determine quickly what the director wants, and how best to show they can deliver it.

In fact, the audition is a two-way communication, and success comes when both actors and directors are aware of each other's needs and common interests. In this book, actors will learn how directors set up auditions and what they're looking for; and how to select and perform monologues, handle cold readings, and work with other performers who are auditioning. Directors will learn how to structure auditions so actors will be able to do their best work, so their casting decisions will ensure a successful production. To provide this insight, the editors of *Stage Directions* magazine have blended our own knowledge of auditions with the expertise of veteran directors and actors in community, regional, and academic theater.

After an overview of the audition process, the book first focuses on how the director shapes and guides that process, including tips on organization, publicity, script readings, callbacks, and casting, as well as gauging the promise or problems that prospective cast members may exhibit. Next, the section for actors includes how to read audition notices, choose monologues or prepare for cold readings (alone or with other actors), and make a solid impression at both auditions and callbacks for both straight plays and musicals.

If you're an actor, you'll want to know what's going through the director's mind as he or she prepares for and conducts auditions. Having that information will enable you to prepare correctly and respond appropriately. If you're a director, you'll find many ideas in the actor's section that you can incorporate into the audition process. Whether you are an actor or director, a veteran of many auditions or a newcomer to the stage, we hope *The Stage Directions Guide to Auditions* provides you with the tools you need to unlock the potential of the auditions process.

About Stage Directions

The majority of the material in this book is based on information that first appeared in the pages of *Stage Directions*, the "practical magazine of theater." Since 1988, *Stage Directions* has published articles on a wide variety of subject matter—not only acting and directing, but also management, publicity, scenic and costume design, lighting and special effects, and much more.

During that time, we've taken a close look at almost every aspect of the audition process. We've put all that advice together in this book, updated and revised as needed, and added introductions that help put the information into perspective.

As we do with our magazine, we'd like to hear your comments on this book or suggestions for future topics in our expanding library of *Stage Directions* books. Please write to us at: *Stage Directions*, 3101 Poplarwood Court, Suite 310, Raleigh, NC 27604.

Stephen Peithman, Editor-in-Chief
Neil Offen, Editor

The Stage Directions Guide to Auditions

Introduction—
Why Do
We Need
Auditions?

*I*t's a simple question: Why do we need auditions?

Simply put, the answer is that auditions are the most efficient way for a director to see, hear, and evaluate a large number of potential cast members in a relatively short period of time.

Auditions may be for individual productions or for an entire season, and the procedures used often differ between the two. Auditions also may be for one theater company or for several (often called "cattle calls"), such as found on the StrawHat circuit or at major theatrical gatherings like the annual Southeastern Theatre Conference meeting. They aren't always just to get into a show, either—they can be to gain admission into a school or university or for acceptance into a summer program. As you might guess, varying audition styles and methods may be used in all these situations.

Auditions for individual shows usually involve reading from the script. The actors may read with other actors throughout the audition process; in other cases, the actors read lines with a staff person, and only at callbacks do actors read with each other. If the company is doing a musical, actors will be asked to sing and perform movement as well.

Because of the large number of people involved, such auditions take more time. However, they do give the director a chance to see the pool of actors at one time, and to compare individual abilities and suitability for the particular parts.

Other companies audition actors for an entire season, rather than play by play. For such auditions, the actor often is asked to prepare two brief monologues—frequently one contemporary and one classic or one dramatic and one comic. If the season includes a musical, actors will be asked to sing and perform movement as well.

Types of Auditions

There are a number of different types of auditions.

- *Open Auditions:* This is the most common type of audition in nonpaid theater. An announcement is posted inviting anyone to attend, and a large group of performers gathers in a rehearsal hall or theater. A three- to four-minute scene is read by different groups of actors, often allowing an actor to try several different roles during the course of the audition. The open audition is a weeding-out exercise in which the director selects those people he or she would like to return for callbacks.

- *Closed Auditions:* Closed auditions usually are open only to a select group (such as students in a particular class or members of a group) or by invitation, and you typically must make an appointment for a specific day and time. Actors may read with other actors or with a member of the director's staff, or even with the director; in that case, there are no other actors present in the audition space. Closed auditions tend to move more quickly than open auditions because fewer people are involved and, therefore, there are fewer distractions. Normally, a director uses the intimate nature of the audition to work more closely with the actor, including making suggestions for alternative line readings or characterization.

Auditions for a musical add a layer or two of complexity. Performers will be asked to sing something appropriate and usually asked to join others in learning a short dance routine, which they then run through for the director and choreographer.

- *Callbacks:* After the first round of auditions, the director generally has a group of potential cast members and wishes to try them out in readings with each other, to check for voice, look, and how one actor might play with and off another. The director calls them back to take a second, more definitive look. Callbacks tend to be more intense because the director is nearing the end of the casting process; final decisions often are made at this point. However, the director also may call one or two actors back for final readings, usually in private.

What the Director Is Looking For

Because auditions are the first step in the casting process (after studying the script and making notes on the characters and style), they must be somewhat general in nature. At this preliminary stage, the director is getting a sense of the available talent from which to choose the cast—or, in the case of auditions for a drama program, the available talent from which to choose the incoming students. However, specific qualities that most directors agree they watch for include:

- Something in the actor's personality that suggests the character
- Voice and ability to project
- Physical appearance and characteristics as they relate to the role
- Ability to focus and take direction if offered
- Stage presence and poise
- A match with the theatrical requirements of the role. For example, if the part calls for someone to "take stage"—that is, dominate the proceedings—the actor should indicate this ability. On the other hand, if the play is an ensemble piece, the actor should indicate an ability to be part of that ensemble.

While the director tries to be as objective as possible, casting decisions are based to a great extent on instinct—the actor's as well as the director's. The more experienced either is, the sharper those instincts tend to be. Certainly, a well-organized director and a well-prepared actor are common interests for everyone involved. The remainder of this book focuses on how those interests can be served best.

Auditions and Actors | 1

*I*nformed and prepared actors have an immediate advantage at the audition. They project confidence, make better choices, and deliver a better reading. They have a far better chance of getting a part.

How to Find Out About Auditions

Make sure you're on the company mailing list. Most companies send out information to members or actors on their list well ahead of public notice. Check company newsletters, websites, and notices in local papers; regional theater organizations also may have an information hotline. Some companies are very good at informing actors of auditions; in other cases, you'll have to assume this responsibility yourself. Create a list of all companies in your area with which you might work, including a contact name and phone number. If the company accepts resumés and photos, be sure yours are on file.

Regional auditions most often are publicized through regional theater associations or theater publications such as

Back Stage. You'll also find general audition information in Jill Charles' annual *Summer Theatre Directory* and *Regional Theatre Directory*, available through bookstores. For the hotlines often provided by organizations, you call a specific number for a recorded list of auditions.

How to Read an Audition Announcement

Read announcements carefully—and read between the lines as well. Determine whether you are qualified or if you meet specific guidelines mentioned in the announcement. Check whether the character rundown fits your own characteristics—physically, emotionally, stylistically. Are you—or could you be—the right age, the right ethnicity, the right personality, the right "type"? Determine whether you would be comfortable playing any of the roles.

Above all, get a copy of the play and read it first. Make sure you know the play and *want* to be in it. (We remember one actor, after being cast as Kate in *The Taming of the Shrew*, announcing to the director that she would be unable to utter the character's famous last speech—"I am ashamed that women are so simple"—because she disagreed with its sexist implication. She should have made this clear before the audition—or simply not tried out for the role in the first place.)

A good audition announcement will give some specifics for each of the characters—age, physical characteristics, personality traits. Study these to see which of the characters fits you best. If the announcement does not give this information, it may be available as a separate handout from the director or company. If there is no specific information, then read the play with particular care. Some scripts give this information up front; in other cases, you'll need to determine it from your own analysis. Take notes, not only of which characters you might be suitable for, but also for personality, motivations, and relationships that might help you better prepare for the auditions.

Remember: The director wants commitment from actors. Those who audition "for the fun of it" or just to "see if I can get a part in a play" are obvious and usually don't get cast. More important, they can waste everybody's time.

Preparation

You can make yourself ready for auditions in several ways. One is through *backgrounding*, which includes a study of the script and the roles up for consideration. Your goal is to get a clear idea not only of the story, but also of the characters and their interrelationships. While you may not know in advance the particular angle the director will take or how he or she sees the play, the more you know about the work, the better off you'll be when you do find out.

Specific preparation depends on the demands of the audition. You may be asked to do *cold readings*—that is, reading a script with no prior exposure to it. Or you may be given portions of the script beforehand and asked to familiarize yourself with it (normally, you're not asked to memorize it). In both cases, you may do the reading with other actors, or (less often) with the director or a member of the director's staff.

The most detailed preparation comes with auditions that demand that you present a monologue or pair of contrasting monologues. See Chapter 9, "Choosing the Right Monologue," and Chapter 10, "Preparing and Performing the Audition Monologue."

At Auditions

You'll find many good tips in the articles "How to Get Cast" (Chapter 2) and "The Big Ones" (Chapter 4). In addition, read Chapter 21, "Eight Things to Look for in Auditions," and Chapter 23, "The Seven Warning Signs of Auditions," for the director's perspective.

Callbacks

As explained in the introduction, callbacks are controlled more tightly and are much more specific in nature than general auditions. If you make it this far, it's clear the director believes you at least have the potential to be a member of the cast. Thus, if you are asked to callbacks, be sure you understand what role or roles you're being considered for and what special preparation may be expected. Also learn the logistics of the callbacks—when you're expected to arrive, the type of reading you will be doing, and anything else you feel will help you do well. If you are being called back for a specific role, make sure you really want that role before accepting the invitation. A director appreciates your honesty. If you're not sure you're capable of handling the role, go anyway—the director has seen something in you that suggests you are.

Notification

Find out how you will be notified—by phone call, letter, or reading a posted announcement—and when. This will save you anxiety and the need to pester someone with repeated phone calls.

A Final Note

When you're finished reading this section, move on to read the information for directors as well. You'll find it helpful to understand the audition process from the other's viewpoint. It is the kind of insider information that may make the difference between being cast or not.

How to | 2
Get Cast

*Each actor—as well as each director, of course—has had differ-
ent experiences during auditions. Each actor approaches each
audition differently—some with trepidation, for instance; some
with tremendous eagerness. That's why so many different people
can offer so many varied tips on how to approach the audition
and make it successful for you. In fact, occasionally the tips
might seem contradictory to each other. That's because each tip
has been formed by the specificity of particular experience and
may or may not be applicable for you and your situation. But
taken together, all the tips that follow point to one overriding rec-
ommendation: Be prepared.*

What You Need to Do to Make a Good Impression Every Time

NANCIANNE PFISTER

*T*he actor was bemused. After his audition, he'd been
invited to callbacks, where he was asked to a second callback. When the casting was completed, he
did not have a role. The director, while pleased with
the actor's work, explained that he did not cast him because
he was too tall.

You might wonder how much taller the actor had grown
between the first audition and the second callback. But the
truth is, most directors make casting choices based on the
appearance of the entire show. If an actor looks out of place,
the overall image for which the director is striving can suffer.
As a performer, you have little control over the vision of the
director.

But what about those things in an audition that you can control? Are you missing out on roles because you've neglected some detail that would show the director how effective you would be in this production? With only minutes to make an impression, the slightest sloppiness can result in your not being cast. Consider these twenty-five audition hints, drawn from our experience and from the advice of directors around the country.

■ *Read the audition notice carefully* so you know what will be expected of you. Will there be cold readings? Do you need to prepare a monologue? If so, how long should it be? Should it come from the script or from another source? Will you be asked to sing? To dance? To work with an animal?

■ *Always find out if you must wear special clothing.* Some plays call for heavy movement or dance, and you can't show your skills in a tight skirt or pants.

■ *Get a script and read it.* Familiarize yourself with the material so you can understand the characters.

■ *If you are asked to prepare something, prepare.* One director told us she felt "insulted" when an actor auditioned for a musical with a song he had not prepared. He may have been under the mistaken impression that since he knew the director he didn't have to impress her. He did impress her, however—negatively. Another director said he had asked all those auditioning to prepare a one-minute monologue. One person got up, rattled on for almost one minute about how she hadn't had time to prepare, then launched into a stop-and-start attempt at her monologue. "If she'd just gone ahead and done the monologue, I might have given her the benefit of the doubt," he said. "But after her long-winded excuses, I was more prepared to murder her than cast her."

■ *Be on time.* Better still, be early. In group auditions, key people usually will be introduced and there will be announcements on audition procedures, on the method of notifying the cast, and on the length of time from auditions to casting completion. You will want to know what's going to happen.

■ *Turn off your electronic pager, cell phone, and wristwatch alarm.* It's only polite. If the other part of your world can't function without you for a couple of hours, a director could wonder how it will survive a rehearsal and performance schedule.

■ *Bring a pen.* There will be forms to fill out. Pencil will smudge and is more difficult to read in a darkened theater. If your handwriting is less than clear, print. No one has time to decode.

■ *List every phone number where you can be reached.* It is amazing how often actors at an audition say they do not wish to divulge their home phone numbers. If you have concerns about your personal safety, get an answering machine and screen your calls. If it's not OK to be called at work, don't list your work number, and tell the casting people why. Also, tell of any plans to be away from home in the next few days. If you can't be found, you won't be cast.

■ *If you're a newcomer to the company, bring a resumé (see Chapter 12).* The degree of formality required varies with each company, but no director will be insulted if handed a clean, thorough, well-prepared resumé. Bringing a resumé does not excuse you from completing the company's required audition form, even though much of the same information will be needed. Your resumé will go into the company files; the audition form is show-specific.

■ *Bring a picture*, especially if you have never auditioned for this company (see Chapter 13). For a professional Actors Equity company, it is, of course, required. For smaller, nonprofessional theaters, a professional headshot would be great, but it is expensive; in some cases, a snapshot will do (ask ahead of time what is expected). The casting people need to remember what you look like. We know a company that takes Polaroid photos of each newcomer—but don't count on that. Do not submit a photograph in costume. That will make it more difficult for a director to imagine you in some other role.

■ *Dress for the role you want.* This doesn't mean be in costume; it means indicating by what you wear that you've done your homework, that you have some idea of the style of the show and the nature of your character. A woman auditioning for the role of a nun is unwise to do so in a frilly or low-cut dress. You may argue that the director should be auditioning you, not your wardrobe. You're right, but auditioning is not about being right. It's about making it as easy as possible for the director to envision you in the part you want.

■ *Prepare!* OK, we've said it once, but it bears repeating. Too many people rely on past performances or experience with directors. These actors develop an attitude: "They've seen me work; I don't have to impress them." Yes, you do. A director may have seen you in the last show, but this is the next show. Instead of resting on your laurels, you should feel challenged to be twice as creative in your audition.

■ *Be creative.* The too-tall actor mentioned previously once had to audition for a director who was a long-time friend. They had directed each other and played opposite each other many times. Rather than think he need not bother to prepare, the performer looked for a way to have the director remember his doing something special. He sang his audition song the way four different characters in the upcoming show might sing it. He did not sing the song four times, but instead changed character throughout the song. To help his audience keep track of the roles, he used 3×5 cards with each character's name on one. As he changed characters, he displayed the appropriate card. This bit of nonsense resulted in a release of tension for the other auditioners, a smile from the director, and a role for the singer.

■ *If you are asked to prepare a monologue or song, be brief.* Too often, actors think they are choosing something for a one-man show or concert. But it's not a concert, it's an audition. Extended arias or songs with multiple verses should be left behind or shortened. In monologues, give yourself just enough time to warm up, then show off your abilities in a few bold strokes. The director will thank you for it.

■ *When auditioning for a musical, prepare a song in the same style as the show*, although not from the same show unless specifically requested to do so. No matter how well you sing that country-western number, it won't show the directors that you can handle a Gilbert and Sullivan patter song.

■ *Talk with the accompanist about your song.* Do you want the second ending? Do you want the high note? (Thinking of singing *a capella* or to taped accompaniment? Don't, unless there is no other option.)

■ *When your name is called, step into the audition space with energy and confidence.* Pause for a few seconds, then say, "Hello. My name is . . . ," then pause again. Since you've just been called by name, why would you do this? It's a way of saying that you are ready and the casting people should pay attention. Don't say, "I'm. . . ." The extra four syllables give the casting crew time to focus on you—to look up from a form they are reading or to finish a comment they are writing. Once you have commanded attention, announce your monologue or song, briefly supplying any background you find necessary to set a mood. If you have edited your selection, now's the time to say so.

■ *Whether you speak or sing, project with the same energy you will use in performance.* If you cannot be heard, what's the point?

■ *Whether you speak or sing, enunciate with the same clarity you will use in performance.* If you cannot be understood, what's the point?

■ *Whether you speak or sing, use the language of the show being cast.* You may be the finest Figaro since Caruso, but if you sing his song, how will the directors judge your diction as Nicely-Nicely Johnson?

■ *Play to the casting team.* If auditions are open for all to watch, you'll have an appreciative and supportive audience, but your fate is not in their hands. Don't ignore them, but address most of your attention to the director, musical director, choreographer, producer, or anyone else who will have a say in casting. Just don't look at them. Many directors find a direct gaze disconcerting.

■ *When you've finished your song or monologue, stay where you are*, waiting for any further requests or instructions. When the director says, "Thank you," return the courtesy and leave the audition space. Remember to thank the accompanist.

■ *Be flexible.* You've read a scene with another actor. Now the director says, "Read it as if you hated each other" or "Read it as if you shared a deep sorrow" or "Read it as if you've just won the lottery." Give it your best shot, no matter how far out of character you feel. No one expects a polished performance; the director wants to know that you can accept direction and will take risks. If the musical director asks you to vocalize to your lowest note, do so without comment or excuse. (At one audition, the director asked a group of people reading a scene to be "as silly as you can be." No one did so. If just one had taken the lead, the rest might have followed. Or if the rest didn't follow, at least the one actor who did as directed would have impressed the director.)

■ *If auditions are open, stay and be part of an audience for the other performers*, as they were for you. Some directors like to add theater games or exercises to an audition, so don't leave until you are certain you will no longer be needed.

■ *If auditions run two nights or more, find out if you can come back and read again.* Some directors don't mind, others do. Don't ask to sing again unless you really think you can do better—if you do the same or worse, you're no better off.

Someone has compared auditions with the worst kind of job interview. You may never be totally at ease, but you can lessen the stress by paying attention to details. Being in control of your audition means you're more likely to be cast—no matter how tall you are.

Improving Your Audition Technique

3

Five Suggestions to Help You Get the Part You Want

DAVID POGUE

T he audition process is a cruel, heartless system that can make you feel rejected, exhausted, and miserable. It's even worse if you're the one auditioning.

Nobody has devised a better system for letting directors and producers envision each applicant, one by one, in the roles to be filled. The only thing wrong with the system is that it relies on human beings—on actors trying desperately to embody the director's vision of the part (with no way of knowing what that is) and on the imagination and patience of the casting committee, which has sat there, probably for days, attempting to remain impartial, friendly, and awake.

As a professional musical director, I've watched more than one director ignore the perfect-for-the-role actress as he unpacks a bag full of delivered Chinese food. Far more often, though, I've seen performers and roles fail to come together because of poor audition technique. Here are a few suggestions on how to improve that technique.

1. *The pianist is your friend.* The pianist can make or break you; treat that pianist accordingly. Be friendly and appreciative. *Briefly* discuss your music. Indicate the tempo you

prefer during a quiet, preperformance meeting; one good way is to softly sing the first line to the pianist.

Come prepared with readable, easy-to-use music whose pages have been taped together. You wouldn't believe the crumbling, disordered music pianists are handed—sometimes the music doesn't include a piano part at all.

2. *Don't dress the part—but hint at it.* If you audition for *Fiddler on the Roof* wearing Russian peasant rags, you'll be laughed out of the room. Yet, wearing clothes and hair that suggest the part can help. If you're auditioning for an executive in *How to Succeed in Business Without Really Trying*, a three-piece suit might be overdoing it, but a shirt and tie would psychologically suggest the part to the audition committee. Theoretically, committee members should be able to imagine that. But in the real world, the less left to the imagination, the better.

3. *What should you do about eye contact?* Some directors love it; they believe you are audience-tuned and your direct appeal satisfies their egos. Others find it annoying and distracting. The safest bet is to make occasional eye contact, but generally direct your presentation just over their heads.

4. *Weird is good, talent is better.* You are aware that the audition committee has seen hundreds of people. You can tell by the bored expressions, the perfunctory "thank-yous." You wish you had been the first or last to audition because people at either end tend to be remembered better. You decide to make an impression, no matter what it takes.

You can't believe how far some have taken this. Once, an actor came up to the audition committee's table, took a long swig from the choreographer's Pepsi and said, "Thanks. Man, was I thirsty." Another spent his audition muttering to himself. I even saw one young woman audition completely naked, in hope of making an impression. (She did; she just didn't get the part.)

Strangeness can make you memorable, but only if there's talent to back it up. You don't want them just to remember you; you want them to remember how good you were.

5. *It isn't just talent.* It's also type. If you didn't get the part, don't be hard on yourself. You may be terrific. Trouble is, casting people don't just want talent; they want talent in the right package (e.g., hair color, height, age, body weight, vocal quality). It's not uncommon

for somebody with the right body type to get the part over somebody with more talent.

See how easy it is? Just be talented, wear the right thing, treat the pianist nicely, make an impression, use the right amount of eye contact, and, above all, be sure you match the director's unspoken mental image of the ideal performer's height, weight, hair color, age, and voice. The part will be yours.

4 | The Big Ones

In addition to the auditions where you are trying out for a particular role or even for several roles during a particular season, there are large group tryouts—called combined auditions—*where you're trying to get a job with one of many summer theater companies or show your talent as a prospective student. (These also are referred to as "cattle calls," often unfairly.) You may be auditioning before a large group of producers, admissions directors, or acting teachers. While much general audition advice still applies, there are also some specific things to know about how to make the best impression at these combined auditions.*

Ten Tips from an Expert to Help You Through Major Auditions

NEAL LEWING

S ummer-stock or season auditions aren't your ordinary song-and-dance. Do your homework in preparing for them or you could wind up selling shoes for the next few months.

With little time to impress a potential employer, an actor must be prepared. Typically, summer tryouts are much more formal, more rigidly structured, and allow far less time for actual presentation than regular auditions. The experience, in other words, can be daunting.

Statewide auditions generally are attended by only a handful of producers, while some of the large regional tryouts—such as those conducted by the Southeastern Theatre Conference or the New England Theatre Conference—may draw as many as thirty, and they can be a tough crowd. You have to impress them even though you may have no more than three minutes onstage: two to present contrasting memorized cuttings and a half-minute to sing to a pretaped accompaniment you provide, unless you are lucky enough to have a live accompanist.

Producers sit stonily around you, jotting hasty notes across your blurred picture and condensed resumé in the photocopied handbook they have been given, then turn mechanically to the next page.

When your time is up, you retire to the green room to wait for the next round. Producers, now assigned to individual meeting rooms, post the name (or number) of performers who interested them on a bulletin board. Then, one at a time, you go into your callback interview where you meet one-on-one to discuss your resumé, financial arrangements, time commitments, and even intimate details about your personality. Depending on the number of callbacks, you may have five to twenty minutes with a would-be boss, so how you handle yourself is vital.

While some summer companies may try to cast from local populations, other professional and semiprofessional theaters represented at state and/or regional auditions often screen several hundred actors over a weekend. To increase your chances of getting considered for summer stock, then hired, and even asked back for next season, here are ten helpful hints gleaned from twenty-five years of personal involvement in summer stock, as well as from other directors and producers. (For that matter, these points are useful in almost *any* general audition.)

1. *Know Yourself.* If you're a five-foot-three, ninety-pound tenor, don't get mad at the director for casting someone else as *Oklahoma!*'s Jud Fry. If you're fifty-five years old and can't carry a tune, why resent the theater for not letting you play Annie (Oakley or Warbucks)? Accept the fact that certain body or age types suggest certain roles. Even if you sing like a nightingale, at six-foot-six and 240 pounds with graying temples, you may be playing mainly villains, father figures, or aged character parts. Directors look for believability onstage, even though an actor has "always wanted to play that role," "knows all the songs by heart," or "played it in high school."

2. *Know What Theaters are Looking For.* Most summer-stock companies produce musicals and contemporary comedies, many in small towns. Summer audiences generally want to laugh, hum familiar tunes, and not dwell on messages. So take the Hamlet soliloquy to Shakespeare company tryouts. David Mamet or Sam Shepard monologues won't help you get a role in *No, No Nanette*. If Neil Simon is on tap, we don't need the monologue about murdering

your mother. Save the drama for drama. Strut your goofy stuff for musicals and comedies.

3. *Concentrate on Your Stage Presence.* Perky smile—that's good. Pleasant singing voice—always a plus. Flawless dance—sounds perfect. But wait. We can see sweaty palms, hesitant movements, and a faltering introduction. Obviously, this actor is not comfortable being onstage with everybody looking at him. You may have wonderful technique, but that can't compensate for missing confidence. The actor we're looking for must exude confidence and show always that he or she is comfortable onstage—no matter what the situation.

4. *Don't Make Excuses.* "I'm sorry. I have a cold so my voice isn't good today." "I'm sorry. My alarm didn't go off this morning, so I'm a little slow." "I'm sorry. My dog ate my music, so I'm a little distracted." Well, we're sorry, too. We were planning to cast someone who could skirt life's little traumas, the kinds of things that surely will arise during a summer show's three-week run. We know it's 8 A.M., and you're number two of two hundred, and your sinuses are draining. But we can spot potential, so just go for it. If you're absolutely too sick to perform for three minutes, write or call, express your interest, or send a videotape. We can't come back later, so don't tell us you'll be able to sing better in two weeks, providing you get cast.

5. *Just Give Us the Facts.* The interview is our chance to get to know you beyond your three-minute routine. Anyone can be charming for ten minutes when employment hangs in the balance, but we want to see the real you now. Because theater is an extraordinary business, we want to know your honest response to extraordinary situations. How do you feel about a daily routine that includes ten hours of rehearsals, tech work, marching in the annual Gooseberry Festival Parade, radio interviews, sharing living quarters with ten other people just like yourself, all for summer theater compensation?

6. *Bring Standard Materials with You.* We're casting two actors. Out of three hundred auditioners, we've called back twenty. Now it's time to collate new names and faces with roles available. Reams of notes cannot take the place of a standard headshot and resumé. Don't forget them. And that resumé should include your credits, certainly, but mention your funky skills as well. Can you juggle? Do rope tricks? Walk on your hands? (We called back one girl because she played the tuba—never used it, but it got our

attention.) We're casting *now*, not in three weeks when you mail us your material.

7. *Pay Attention to Your Appearance.* Sit up straight, look us in the eye, and speak clearly. Get some sleep the night before. Comb your hair. And be prepared for anything. With a great number of auditioners to see, we may have time only to note you as "the girl in the baggy green sweater." On the other hand, don't be so outrageous that you are reduced simply to a giant question mark felt-penned across your bio. As an actress you have every right to exercise your individuality, but don't imagine a potential employer isn't going to be affected by the rips in your old jeans, pizza smudges on your shirt, and the nose ring. You will represent the good name of our theater and the art form itself. Originality is to be applauded, but remember, we're going to be marketing you to the theater-going public. We appreciate a professional appearance and demeanor as much as any job interviewer.

8. *Be Professional—Even Behind the Scenes.* We're not just evaluating you during the audition itself and the interview. We're evaluating you whenever we see you—in the hotel lobby or in the coffee shop. We attended auditions one year in a brand new state-of-the-art facility. To get to the stage, all the directors had to walk through the green room where the auditioners nervously waited. One actor in particular impressed us right away. He was telling a loud, off-color joke, slopping a cup of coffee in one hand, shoving the girl next to him like a first grader. I know I shared the other directors' instant opinion before the fellow ever took the stage.

9. *Show You Can Be Part of a Team.* We look for actors who are multitalented, naturally, but who also are not afraid to get paint under their fingernails and can work effectively with others. Everyone must function as an equal member of the team. In other words, we don't want to see you acting like a star. The show does not revolve around your performance and the chain of company morale stretches thin at the weakest link. Word spreads quickly from company to company. If you have an attitude that causes friction, we'll know by next season. Most directors agree that casting is fifty percent for talent, fifty percent for compatibility.

10. *Don't Keep Us Hanging.* We want you to come work for us. We have a contract right here for you to sign *today*. You know what we're looking for and what's expected of you, now let's talk about what we can offer you. But you want to wait to hear from two other theaters? You can let us know in four to six weeks? It sounds like

you're holding out in case a better offer comes in the mail tomorrow. Or you can't make up your mind in less than a month? (Will you need extra time to learn your lines, too?) If you're interested, tell us now. There are hundreds of potential actors out there who would be happy for an offer, so let's be fair to everyone.

As you should understand by now, auditioning—particularly for a summer-stock job—is a very specialized kind of stage work that demands as much skill and determination as playing a role in any show. You have to keep working at it.

Advice from a College Recruiter | 5

Some of the biggest of the big ones, some of the most nerve-wracking auditions, are held at the summer festivals where potential college scholarships are on the line. Here are an insider's tips for students on how to succeed at summer festivals when the pressure is on.

How to Get Noticed— and Maybe Snag a Scholarship

NANCIANNE PFISTER

You've finished your junior year of high school and you want a career in the theater. Training is mandatory, but expensive. A scholarship will help and you hope to get one through auditions at summer theater festivals. How do you improve your chances? How can your teacher help?

"Auditioning is the most unnatural thing actors do. Young actors especially must understand it doesn't just happen; you must practice doing it."

That's Rule Number One, as offered by Roberta Rude, head of the Department of Theatre at the University of South Dakota. I spoke with her shortly after she returned from the International Thespian Festival, held annually at the University of Nebraska's Lincoln campus.

Sponsored by Thespians, the high-school theater organization, the Lincoln event is typical of other scholarship festivals held throughout the country. While no definite offers of assistance are made at the festival, students and college representatives get a chance to meet and share information. Students are then given a festival application to return to the school of their choice. Chances of success are high. At the University of South Dakota, for instance, five students competing at one recent festival each were offered $1,000 scholarships.

Almost 2,700 people attended that festival, and more than 300 high school students auditioned for scholarships. Colleges send their representatives to these festivals to recruit for their departments. What grabs their attention? Rude offers some frontline advice.

Before you set foot on the stage, she says, it is important to fill out the application form correctly and completely. Forgetting to list a preference for a B.A. or B.F.A. program is confusing. The B.A. is a general degree of 30–40 units; it may leave you time for a double major. The B.F.A. is an intense study requiring 78 units; it leaves you time for little else. College recruiters need to know your preference.

Failing to include your GPA, your class standing, or your PSAT scores will raise suspicions. No matter how talented you are, no college will grant you a scholarship if you are unlikely to meet the overall graduation requirements. Offer explanations for any response that might raise questions. Like all such applications, this one must be legible and neat.

The paperwork finished, you must choose your audition piece. Ask your drama coach for help. At Lincoln, students had four minutes in which to shine. Elsewhere, 90 seconds is the maximum audition time allowed. Rude is not dismayed by this: "I've called back students because of 20 seconds that grabbed me." She advises choosing a short piece that allows you to demonstrate a range of abilities rather than a longer piece that may force you to rush through it.

Rude also cautions against singing. Most colleges don't offer musical theater majors, so the student wanting such training would double-major in drama and music. The university theater people want to see you act; save your singing for an audition with a music department. If you have time for two short pieces, you are better off showing two contrasting styles of acting rather than including a song. Never do two songs.

Age-appropriateness is one of the first considerations in choosing audition material, according to Rude. It's not that every student is stuck being Tom Sawyer or Anne of Green Gables; it's that few students have the experience required for a credible portrayal of Blanche Dubois or Lady Macbeth. Generally, do not do Shakespeare; those for whom you are auditioning most likely will have seen it done better by an experienced performer and you will suffer by comparison. For the same reason, avoid the Greek classics. If you feel compelled to use them, find a very good modern translation, Rude advises.

Make the final decision about your audition material a year in advance. You need that much time to study it and live with it so it's yours. If you use new material, you risk losing focus while you worry about forgetting a line. College recruiters want to know you are in control.

Analyze the material thoroughly, Rude says. Work with your teacher to pay attention to the language. What does this mean? Why does the character use these words?

Perform your piece in as many places as you can so you learn to scale it for your voice and the space you are in. Use different stages, different lights. This does not always need to be a formal staging area. Rude advises: "If you're walking through a building and come to an open space, stop and perform your audition piece. If someone sees you, that's not unlike what may happen elsewhere."

Teachers can be a big help in providing such opportunities, according to Rude. "Coaches can use meetings or class time for rehearsal of audition pieces," she explains. "Send students elsewhere on the spur of the moment: a stage, outdoors, the local mall. If they can't leave the campus, choose another classroom, a lab, even a closet—anything to test the material in a new space. Teachers also can use class time for mock auditions. Getting honest feedback from peers about such basics as volume and diction helps each student. It's just as necessary to acknowledge the things that were done well."

Choosing what to wear is far less complicated than it is made out to be, according to Rude. The rule is simple: dress in something either appropriate to the character you'll portray or appropriate to your own personality. Additionally, don't wear anything that hangs loosely; you'll want to show how well you can move. Avoid black. You're likely to be against black drapes and you'll get lost.

"Once your name has been called, remember that you shape the audition from the moment you stand up. The college representatives are not looking for perfection, but for raw talent, for an instrument that can be trained. When you introduce yourself, let it be known you have something special to offer, that you really are glad to be there and are happy to share what you have with them. You have set the stage for a nice exchange."

Rude admits that watching auditions for nearly five hours a day for three days can be "mind-numbing." Still, of the 300 applicants she saw, she called back 80 for interviews. She cautions students not to feel they will get lost in the crowd.

"You have to remember that even at the end of a very long day," she says, "we want you to be fabulous!"

Fighting Stage Fright | 6

Auditions are intimidating. You are nakedly putting yourself on the line, asking to be judged, frequently by people you've never seen before. There is, by definition, no place to hide. In almost no other field of endeavor are your emotions so close to the surface and your every action so minutely analyzed. It is not surprising, then, that many actors develop stage fright during auditions. But there are ways of dealing with it.

How to Avoid and Overcome "Performance Anxiety"

Lani Harris

*I*f you are one of the lucky few who have never felt the mind-numbing panic of what's technically called "performance anxiety," congratulations. But don't get too comfortable—like the flu, stage fright has been known to hit anybody at anytime.

Even Sir Laurence Olivier, at the peak of his accomplishments, developed a case of overwhelming stage fright. Judging from the overflow attendance at my performance-anxiety workshops around the country, and the number of actors I have seen freeze from nerves at auditions, in class, and onstage during fifteen years of teaching, directing, and adjudicating for competitions, I feel it's clearly not a rare problem. That's why every actor should learn how to cope with stage fright so that it will not be debilitating when it hits. If it hits during an audition, obviously, there goes any chance you might have of getting cast.

Here are six tips that can help if you are suddenly seized by performance anxiety.

1. *Focus.* Fear is a distraction. You have stopped focusing on your character's goal and begun to think about something else. That might be getting the words right or whether your fly is open. You have become "self"-conscious. You are no longer "in the moment" as the character, and it shows.

Obviously, not *all* distractions will lead to fear, but when an actor begins to focus on the fear, to concentrate on it, that distracts from the character. Actors without something to do, without something to focus on, can appear uncomfortable. Sometimes, they won't make eye contact or will develop nervous mannerisms or show defensive postures. They will start to become anxious.

On the other hand, when you have something to focus on, there will be a noticeable physical relaxation, a reduction or disappearance in nervousness. When given something to focus on, you no longer are thinking about the audience, and that makes a big change in your appearance. Your body relaxes and responds in a very natural way that can be read by anyone watching you.

If you start to become distracted during auditions (and it's easy to do), immediately focus on the scene. Ask yourself "Who am I?," "What do I want?," and "How badly do I want it?" Bring yourself back into your character, focus on the character's intention/goal. Even if you lose a line, this way will allow you to create a sensible ad-lib.

Often, physically connecting with your environment will help. Can your character straighten the papers on the desk? Smooth a jacket? Nothing big or distracting, and always in character, physical contact can heighten your focus on the character.

2. *Breathe.* When an actor becomes focused on fear, panic may develop. A message is received by your brain and a very primal response is triggered, known as the *fight-or-flight response.* This enabled primitive humans to either fight the enemy or run away as the bloodstream was flooded with a powerful chemical: adrenalin.

An excess of adrenalin, though, is not likely to help you at auditions. It causes all kinds of physical symptoms: dry mouth, throat tightening, sweaty palms, thundering heartbeat, nausea, dizziness, bladder urgency, shaking, rapid speech, vocal changes, twitches, spasms, and a loss of memory.

You also are more likely to tighten your chest and actually hold your breath when you feel fear, causing a lack of oxygen to the brain. That has two immediate results: disorientation and paranoia, the last two things you need at an audition.

When you feel any of these symptoms, the best thing to do is breathe properly. Oxygen will dilute the adrenalin in your bloodstream, your brain will clear, and your body will start to relax.

The key is to stay aware; if you notice any of the warning signs, take slow, deep breaths. This will allow you to take control of the situation and the audience won't know. And at the same time you are doing this, force yourself to focus.

These first two steps can be used during that moment onstage when fear hits, but there are steps you can take before you are in performance that also will help.

3. *Prepare.* This may sound obvious, but it is worth mentioning. None of these techniques will make up for lack of preparation. In auditions, know what will be expected of you; be ready with your monologue. In a show, know your lines, your blocking, your cues. Be prepared.

4. *Define Your Fear.* When dread is building up prior to an audition, define exactly what you are afraid of. What is the worst that could happen? Be very specific.

You will muff a line or a reading? Then what? Very likely someone will cover. You will ad-lib. Or the stage manager will give the line. But something *will* happen. What else? You will faint? Then what? Someone will drag your unconscious carcass offstage and probably slap you or throw water in your face. What else? You will throw up? Then what? A very annoyed stagehand will have to clean it up. What else? You wet your pants? *Then what?* Your drycleaner will kill you.

Are you laughing yet? The key here is to name each fear, asking yourself "Then what?" Carry this out until it's funny. One of the best ways of reducing the power of your fears is to laugh at them. And by defining what you are afraid of, you can figure a way out. You can prepare a solution to each problem.

5. *Visualize the Good.* In great detail, precisely imagine everything going well. Visualize success. Go over that image in your mind until it is deeply ingrained. Too often we spend our time visualizing what we are afraid of, and that image gets recorded on our subconscious.

Instead, see yourself doing everything perfectly, overcoming each problem. Spend as much time with positive images as you can. Refuse to let an image of fear become established.

6. *Use the Energy.* This technique can be a lifesaver, but will not work in every circumstance. It also does not mean you let the adrenalin take over, creating a manic performance, words shooting out like a machine gun. This approach takes thought and control.

For whatever reason, there may come a time when you are not able to fully overcome your nerves, panic, or a personal emotion that has hold of you. Say, for example, moments before the audition or a performance, the love of your life calls and breaks up with you. Or you get word that someone close to you has died. What can you do? You can try to find a parallel between what is happening to your character and the emotions you are feeling. Channel all the energy into your character's goals or objectives. This will heighten the stakes and give you a point of concentration, rather than letting your feelings become a distraction.

When I was a struggling actress in Los Angeles, I was very late for the taping of a video project, due to circumstances beyond my control. Although it was explained to the director and he was willing to wait for me, by the time I got there I was completely unnerved. Overwhelmed with worry about making a bad impression in a professional situation, I felt panic about the taping.

I had to find a way to focus. I looked for a parallel between what I was feeling and the part I was playing. The monologue that had been assigned for the taping was from *Anne of a Thousand Days*, the speech before Anne is taken to the gallows. At that moment, I could certainly relate to being killed in public. This connection allowed me to take all my personal anxiety and use it, in character, to fuel the speech. Using this technique gave me a way to perform successfully and I received other jobs as a result of that performance. As I said, it doesn't always work in every situation, but sometimes it can really turn things around.

Try to practice and repeat these six specific steps to become so familiar with them that they are automatic. As you practice and find that these steps really work, your confidence will increase, knowing you can control the fear and that stage fright does not have to get in the way of your performance—at auditions or in the full glare of the spotlight.

Warming Up the Voice | 7

Just as you would do for any performance, it's a good idea to warm up for any audition, too. And that includes warming up your physical instrument, particularly your voice.

How to Prepare Your Instrument Before You Must Use It

"There is no one right way to breathe," says voice coach Bonnie Raphael. "But it's also true that a lot of actors don't breathe properly."

A teacher and vocal coach since 1965, Raphael's opinion carries the weight of experience. She has worked with the American Repertory Theatre of Cambridge, Massachusetts, the University of Virginia, and, most recently, PlayMakers Repertory at the University of North Carolina, Chapel Hill.

Raphael works with people to "develop their *own* voice, to answer whatever dramatic demands there may be. Your voice is your voice. How you use it depends on the needs of the role. But in order to use your voice effectively, you have to treat it with respect."

Basic to Raphael's method is a twenty- to twenty-five-minute warmup before an audition, rehearsal, or performance, plus a shorter warmdown afterwards. Too many actors shy away from warmups, which she thinks is a sin.

"They think it's 'wussy' or they feel silly. That's something you just have to get over. Just do it. The second-worst sin is doing the same warmup, summer or winter, whether you're playing a major role with lots of lines or a small role with only a few. You need to design your warmup for the space you're in, the show you're in, the role you're playing—and how you feel, emotionally and physically, at the moment."

To determine how much warmup is needed, Raphael suggests beginning by "checking-in."

"Go some place quiet, stand and close your eyes. Just check-in and see how you're feeling, emotionally and physically. Excited or tired? Are you breathing hard or holding it in anticipation? Any signs of a sore throat or allergy? Where's your tongue—on the roof of your mouth or down where your lower jaw is? Do your feet hurt? Observe, don't judge, how you're feeling. Just acknowledge where you are."

You will now be able to use your warmup time to best advantage, focusing on where there is tension. You also will be able to determine how to accommodate your energy level to that of the parts for which you may audition.

The Home Stretch

After checking-in, it's time to stretch, using ambient or other quiet music to help actors focus.

"A body that is stiff and frozen will produce a voice that is stiff and frozen, and a characterization that is stiff and frozen," Raphael says. She suggests that actors yawn, then stretch legs, arms, and shoulders. Do this slowly, however—no lunges or quick movements.

"Close your eyes for a moment and create more space by dropping your jaw and loosening the area between the shoulder blades. Pay attention to the joints, your rib cage. Bring the arms up slowly as if strings were pulling them to shoulder level, then let the fingers stretch out."

After stretching to ambient music, she suggests switching to something with a stronger beat. "Using rhythm is very important. It helps get you into moving, which you'll have to do onstage, and helps relieve muscle tension. I like to choose music especially for the production that helps warm me up and that prepares me for that particular show. It becomes identified in my mind with going onstage."

Again, it's important to keep this and all exercises gentle. "If it is loose, it will shake. If it's not relaxed, it will not shake. So this is a good diagnostic to find out where your body is tense. Then use the rhythm to move and loosen it. Start with the feet, then move to the legs, thighs, trunk, arms, hands, shoulders, neck, the jawbone."

Limbering the Voice

Once actors are more relaxed, they need to make sure that breathing is regular and deep.

"When you breathe from the upper chest, you risk straining the voice," Raphael explains. "And you can see the tension in an actor who takes shallow breaths. You can see the muscles pulling all the way up into the jaw. So try to breathe as low down in the chest as you are comfortable doing. There's no magic spot. It's different with each person. A good exercise is to lie on the floor. When you breathe in this position, it goes right into the back. Notice that this is where your muscles want to work. So just let yourself fill with air, then sigh it out. Fill up the back, then sigh it out."

Limbering up the mouth and jaw muscles is also important.

"Take a deep breath and make a motorboat sound to relax the lips. Then move from the motorboat to a hum in one movement. Don't push it, though. Remember that loudness is not volume. If you push the voice, you'll strain it. From the audience perspective, 'loudness' has more to do with resonance, clarity, articulation, and phrasing. The audience sometimes will say they can't hear, but that doesn't mean the voice is necessarily too soft. A good actor can be understood even when being relatively quiet."

She suggests going from the motorboat sound to an open "la-la," in which the mouth opens slowly from the back to change the sound. At the end, the tongue rests behind the upper teeth as the actor goes "la-la-la" (i.e., "brrrrr-aah-la-la-la-la-la-la").

After loosening the jaw and lips, Raphael suggests working on variety of pitch. "Start a sigh up high, then go all the way down to the lowest place you have pitch. Don't growl—the low notes should be where you can comfortably speak. Do that a couple of times to get the flow. Then take any speech you're working on and say it this way in half-tone progressions."

After the top-to-bottom sigh, she demonstrates by reciting in her lower register, moving up the scale a few lines at a time: "Speak the speech, I pray you [up], as I pronounce it to you, trippingly on the tongue [up] but if you mouth it, as many of your players do [up]," and so on.

"Do this until you're all the way to the top of your range. If you run out of text before you run out of notes, start the text again. If you run out of notes before you run out of text, drop down again and start another round. Remember, the low notes are not on the floor and the high notes are not on the ceiling. And target the speech to something in the room, so you develop your projection at the same time.

"When you're done, recite the speech in the normal way," she says, "but listen for ways in which that speech can now inhabit different parts of your vocal range. You'll find notes you don't normally use in your voice. When you speak the speech again, twice as many pitches are accessible as they were before."

Throughout the warmup and warmdown (and audition), Raphael advises that actors have plenty of water handy. "It's very, very important to work lubricated. If your mouth is feeling dry, your vocal chords are probably dry as well, and that's damaging to the voice. The amount of water is less important than the frequency of sipping. So have water around at audition, rehearsal, and performance, especially when the air is dry."

Putting the Toys Away

After you have used your voice strenuously, it's important to warm down, just as an athlete does. "I'm of the belief that the best time to get rid of any damage you may have done to the voice—by straining, by overdoing it, by over-enthusiasm, by overwork—is immediately following," Raphael explains. "Not the next morning, when you start getting hoarse, but as soon as you've done the damage. Put the toys back where they were before you started playing with them, particularly after a very strenuous audition, rehearsal, or performance."

Many of the same stretching exercises used in the warmup can be used. "Think of it as restoring balance," she explains. "Do a post-check. Close your eyes and check in. Feeling a little dry? Sip some water. Neck still a bit stiff? Perhaps another few head rolls. Your body will tell you what's needed if you just pay attention."

The muscles of the neck and jaw tend to get the most stress in acting because that's where the tension is, in holding up the head. Actors need to relieve tension there and in the jaw muscle, as well. Shake out the jaw and lips while saying "ahhhhhh," then follow with a sixteen-count head roll.

"Let the jaw drop as you do the head roll," Raphael advises. "Then reverse. Stop with your ear at your shoulder. Then nod up and down, dropping your jaw. You'll feel any tense muscles. Pause at the moment of greatest stretch. Lift the shoulder. Work with the muscles and stretch where you need to."

She also suggests humming softly in the middle of the range and chewing as you do to help relax the jaw muscles.

"Do another check-in to see if you have any residual tension. Stretch or shake it out before you go. Acknowledge that you have returned to your own self. You'll go home refreshed and you'll rest better."

Now You're Talking! 8

After you've warmed up your voice, do you know how to use it best? Do you know how to make the most of it, use it to make an impression on those watching you audition? Voice coach Bonnie Raphael has some suggestions.

How to Use Your Voice to Create Stronger Characters

"*I* don't like the idea of an 'acting voice,'" says Bonnie Raphael. "Your voice is your voice. How you use it depends on the needs of the role."

We watched Raphael work with two actors during a New York City workshop sponsored by the American Association of Community Theatre. Raphael's practical, easily grasped suggestions for breathing and posture helped these two actors create stronger characterizations on the spot—which is, after all, the goal you seek at an audition. One of her subjects was a teenager with limited experience and the other was a working professional. At the end of the workshop, they both were able to deliver their monologues in a more powerful manner—just like you hope to do at an audition.

Focused Energy

Steve, a professional actor, delivered a monologue from *Daddies*, a play by Douglas Gower. It's an in-your-face rant, full of profanity, about a street-corner Santa screaming at a passerby. He presents it in similar fashion, leaning toward the audience, often shouting the lines.

Afterwards, Raphael praises Steve's energy and his understanding of the character. But she also notes his dependence on what she calls the "naturalistic crouch."

"We often fall into this when we're being dramatic," she explained. "The body hunches forward as we try to make eye contact with the audience or another player. But it cramps the stomach muscles and stretches the throat forward. That means not enough air gets out, and the throat has to work harder to project sound."

She also points out a tendency to address a character or the audience through the top of his eyes.

"It's a bad habit, especially with taller actors like Steve. When you look through the top of your eyes, you lower your head and your chin presses on the vocal area. This compromises the relationship between the muscles of the chest and the throat. Actually, the top of your head should be parallel with the ceiling," she explains. "If your eyes were car headlights, the beams would go straight out."

When Steve does his monologue again, without the crouch and looking straight out, it is with greater intensity. Raphael next works on getting a greater feeling of spontaneity into his reading. She suggests three things.

"First, ask yourself the question to which the first line in your monologue is the answer," Raphael begins. "That's what propels you into the monologue. Acting is reacting: A character is speaking because he can no longer remain silent, not because the author has given him a speech. You must provide the trigger, and knowing the answer to that question sets the rhythm of the speech—and that tells you how to use your voice."

Her second suggestion is to "talk *to* [an imaginary] someone, not *at* them—focus your attention *and* your voice for maximum effect."

Her third piece of advice takes Steve by surprise: Raphael asks him to pant. "Start by getting a nice easy pant going. It doesn't have to be big—don't push it," she explains. "Start panting and then go right into the speech. And every couple of lines, pause and start panting again. Don't pant from the throat, though. Keep it down in the torso. Otherwise, it's hard on the voice."

Steve does the scene again, and the panting makes him sound as though fresh from a defensive encounter, which is precisely the situation.

"Of course, you can't pant in every speech," Raphael says, "but you can find something in your speech pattern or breathing pattern that you can use. And you can do it so subtly that the audience isn't aware of what you're doing—even though they will notice the energy this brings to the performance."

As proof, she makes up a speech: "[breath] . . . and this is what I want to tell you [breath] and I've been meaning to tell you this [breath] for twenty-five years."

"Note how that tiny breath prevents you from setting your rhythm and making the speech predictable," she continues. "It prevents you from getting stuck in any particular rhythm." She points out that Steve was every bit as intense with the panting, but without having to shout or lean forward for effect. "It's coming through the voice," she says. "Sometimes actors give a little cake and a lot of icing. What you want is more cake and less icing."

Hide and Seek

Raphael moves on to Rachel, a high school student who performs a dramatic monologue about a teen in anguish. The performance is strained, in part due to nervousness. The angst comes through, but like Steve's first run-through, it's all at the same level. There's no shading. And like many teens, Rachel tends to drop words at the end of phrases. Raphael compliments Rachel's intensity, then points out that, like Steve, she is pushing too hard.

"You're not trusting your voice or you're not trusting your acting enough," Raphael says. "The more the voice does, the more message it carries, and the less extra physical stuff you have to do. A lot of the work I do with my students is simplifying, peeling away the layers. Less is more. Actors have to trust the audience will get it."

Raphael next suggests that Rachel focus more on projecting to the audience. "A lot of your speech was delivered to the floor," she explains, "but the monologue is directed to your mother. In order for us to see you—and, after all, this is an audition piece—you need to direct your speech out, to a place where everyone in the audience can see you and feel included. When I audition, I usually direct myself to a person—real or not—over the shoulder of the person who's doing the auditioning."

When actors work with heavy emotional material, it's important not to hide. "We have to fight that tendency, because in real life we often don't want to face someone when we're upset," Raphael says. "But onstage, you don't want to get lost."

Rachel repeats the monologue. Now, looking out to the audience, she comes closer to realizing the intensity of the moment. Still, something is missing. She knows it and the audience knows it. Raphael gives it a name. Walking up to Rachel as she's delivering a line, Raphael takes Rachel's hand and places it on the young woman's breastbone.

"Notice that you're breathing in the upper chest and throat," she says. "This happens with a lot of actors: As soon as the emotion goes up, so do the shoulders. If you move your shoulders upward when you take a breath, it's a sign you're not breathing correctly. A deep breath expands from the lower chest. A good rule to follow: the higher the emotion, the deeper the breath."

Raphael demonstrates a quick trick for directors to help actors get the breath lower in the body.

"Take a lightweight wooden chair and have the actor hold it above her head with both hands. Don't lock the elbows—allow them to bend slightly. Have her do some deep breathing, then have her say her speech. It makes it impossible to raise the shoulders. The weight of the chair pushes the shoulders down, grounding the actor."

Rachel tries it and the speech improves. There's more variety of pitch, but when she finishes a few lines with the chair overhead, she admits, "I feel stupid."

Raphael nods. "It may feel stupid the first time, but keep at it," she tells the directors in the audience. "After they've done it, do it again, but have them put the chair down halfway through the speech. If the upper body gets very busy again, have them put the chair back up. Eventually, they can keep that feeling of being grounded without the chair."

Raphael next shows Rachel how to breathe from the diaphragm so her words don't drop off at the end of phrases. "The diaphragm is right under the lungs," she explains, placing Rachel's hand on the spot. "Interwoven with the diaphragm is the *solar plexus*, a network of nerves second only to the brain. The solar plexus is thought to be connected with the primitive emotions—grief, rage, lust. When we work on breathing from the diaphragm, we also warm up that network of nerves that allows us to convey emotion in our speech."

How do you know when you are breathing from the diaphragm?

"Do enough aerobic exercise to make you out of breath," Raphael suggests. "You are now breathing from your diaphragm. Put your hand on your stomach and notice that it expands when you inhale. Your neck and shoulders are free. To do the work of an actor, you must breathe from the diaphragm. It provides the power that will project your voice and your character."

Noting Rachel's nervousness, and a monologue that demands she jump immediately into an emotional outburst, Raphael suggests what she calls *bookending*.

"Bring something with you—a small prop to help bookend the

experience. When the prop is there, you're playing the character. When you finish playing the character, you put the prop away. You're creating a beginning and an ending, which is very important when you're playing a role that calls for deep emotions. You literally step into the role and then you step out of it, so you don't wake up at four in the morning with the character's feelings sweeping over you. You need to make a dividing line between you and the part you're playing."

Using techniques such as bookending is a major part of Raphael's approach, which focuses on more than voice and speech. "Eighty percent of my work is changing the mind-set," she explains. "Shakespeare wrote, 'All things are ready if the mind be so,' and I believe that's true.

"Eventually, as you strip away your bad habits, you will come to a point when you'll ask yourself, 'How do I know I'm acting?' Some people 'know' they're acting when they stand a certain way, or their eyes go wild, or their jaws clench. Without these cues, we also take away the comfort we had that we were 'acting.' We feel naked."

But when actors strip away the bad habits and get to the essence of the moment, Raphael says, "We don't have to push. We don't have to 'act.' It's just there."

9 | *Choosing the Right Monologue*

If you're not going to be doing a cold reading, what's the most important decision you can make in preparing for an audition? (That is, after you've warmed up.) Why, choosing which monologue you will perform. There are a multitude of sources to help you choose that monologue—collections of monologues for men, for women, about Elvis Presley, about baseball, about almost any subject and in any form you could imagine. And, of course, you could choose a monologue that hasn't yet been collected into book form, but that you found yourself through your reading.

So, which one to choose? And what to do with it after you make your selection? The next few articles offer some clues.

How to Select Material to Help You Get That Part

GERALD LEE RATLIFF

A "winning" audition monologue involves much more than just basic understanding of the script or performance technique. Too many actors make the fatal error of selecting audition monologues because they like them or because they are "well known." They forget that the primary objective of an audition is to demonstrate a performance personality capable of achieving the vocal and physical character portrait the director has in mind.

The monologue must project a stage presence that is memorable for its inventiveness and promotes the spirit of the character being performed in an honest, natural, and spontaneous way—in a time frame of three to five minutes! Consequently, it's essential to select a monologue that is appropriate and suitable to both the actor's talents and the director's casting needs.

Here are some tips for selecting audition monologues that will help you make a memorable impression and win a positive audition response:

- Suit the monologue to the specific audition call in terms of character type (that is, age, height, weight, and so on).
- Suit the monologue to the character role being sought (for example, mood, attitude, point of view).
- Avoid performance dialects that are not authentic and well defined.
- Avoid "new" audition monologues that have not been refined in an actual performance.
- Make use of the acting edition of a script compiled specifically for performance.
- Make use of contrasting audition monologues that indicate your experience, range, and versatility (e.g., verse, prose, serious, comic, classical, or contemporary).
- Select an audition monologue that includes a vivid character portrait revealing one or more climactic moments, a series of striking turning points, conflict (internal or external), and a range of emotional, intellectual, or psychological qualities.
- Choose a monologue with a beginning, middle, and end—a structured sequence of events that allows the character in a brief period to express a point of view, develop a sense of direction, and pursue a course of action that ultimately is resolved in a climactic incident of some intensity.
- Don't select audition monologues that primarily rely on crucial costumes, props, set pieces, or sound effects to visualize the selected character. Remember that an essential ingredient in the audition process is for you to "act" material revealing vocal and physical range, rather than to accentuate the material with extraneous accessories that may clutter the playing area or detract from your audition performance.

Additional Dimensions

There are a number of significant additional dimensions to consider in selecting winning audition monologues that may have the potential for an inventive performance.

1. Look for an audition monologue that encourages a personal signature—an immediate identification with the character's given circumstances, mood, attitude, and reaction or response to the situation being described.

2. Look for an audition monologue that encourages instinctive acting and making bold, daring performance choices that build moment-to-moment anticipation and suspense.

3. Look for an audition monologue that has a "tempo" that underscores the attitude or the mood of the character for its most immediate impact.

4. Look for an audition monologue that actively engages both voice and body in mental and physical characterization.

5. Choose a monologue that suggests the "here and now" in terms of appropriate bodily actions, gestures, and movement to clearly visualize a fresh, original character portrait.

Supplementary Sources

Although the primary source of performance materials is still found in anthologies of scenes and monologues edited especially for auditions, other supplementary sources are available for the imaginative actor to consider, including song lyrics, film scripts, short stories, and historical biographies or diaries. Occasionally, recordings of playscripts, television dramas or comedies, and musical theater soundtracks provide audition monologues rich in personal association and sensitivity. Attending plays also can help you identify potential monologues that might be appropriate for the audition process.

Remember, however, that the winning monologue is the one that feels comfortable, the one that promotes a well-defined use of body and voice similar to your own age and range. The final challenge of the audition is selecting material that is conversational in tone of delivery and that suggests a natural, relaxed sense of "open communication" of your own personality so the character portrait appears both authentic and believable.

Preparing and Performing the Audition Monologue

Making Good Choices Is Step One

Jean Schiffman

10

N owadays, more and more theaters are requiring the standard three-minute audition piece: one or two prepared monologues, maybe a song. In audition listings in one recent trade magazine, ten small and community groups asked for prepared pieces; only five asked for cold readings. No matter where you audition, if prepared pieces are required, the rules are pretty much the same.

Choosing Material

It's always best to do two contrasting pieces if you can (but start with your strongest). Look for material that is emotionally compelling and allows you to go through an emotional transition, advises actor-teacher Ed Hooks, author of *The Ultimate Scene and Monologue Sourcebook*.

"Be comfortable with the language," advises American Conservatory Theatre casting director Meryl Shaw. "Can you wrap your tongue around those syllables? Can you 'speak the speech' clearly and easily?"

Choose material that is appropriate for you chronologically (don't do *King Lear* if you're twenty years old) and temperamentally (if you're a good comedian, for heaven's sake, do something comic). The idea is to show off your best skills—and, within that, to show some range.

Where to find the material? Browse in bookstores. Look for a piece that stands on its own out of context. Most (but not all) directors we talked with agreed: Writing your own audition monologue is very risky. It is harder to be a good playwright than a good actor. Most also agreed that lifting monologues from fiction doesn't work. A novel is meant to be a novel.

Many actors choose provocative pieces—racist or sexist characters, overtly sexual or violent material, profanity. They hope to make an impression. The directors we talked with were, in general, unenthusiastic.

"Aggression is easy to do and tiresome to watch," says Meg Patterson, former casting director at San Jose Repertory Theatre.

"I'm fine with characters that are racist or sexist—but, out of context, sometimes the more sexual monologues seem cheap," warns Amy Potozkin, casting director for the Berkeley Repertory Theatre.

Robert Kelley of Palo Alto's TheatreWorks speaks for all directors when he emphasizes that he's looking for a likeable person as well as a good actor. Your choice of monologue says a lot about you. "If you choose two axe-murderer monologues," Kelley says, "I'll wonder if you're secretly trying to tell us something."

One final word on in-your-face choices: Jill Charles, artistic director of the Dorset Theatre Festival in Vermont, and publisher of a variety of theater directories and resource books, polled a large group of producers who attended East Coast regional auditions. Their biggest complaint was monologues that are "ugly to listen to"—foul language, tirades, "squashed-puppy" speeches, stomach-churners.

Every year, certain monologues tend to be popular among actors and so are either very boring to the auditors or disadvantageous to the actor, who constantly will be compared to the others who did the same piece. It's also a bad idea to choose a monologue from a play that is currently being given a good production at a major theater in your area. One director recommends avoiding recently published books of audition scenes and monologues.

Preparing

Get a coach. (Ask around, check out the trade journals, green-room bulletin boards, your local college drama department.) Don't rely on friends, even if they're actors, for informed feedback. Do, however, rely on friends, your husband, your mother, your cat to provide an audience while you memorize and practice your monologue from here to next Sunday.

Keep in mind that acting and auditioning are birds of a different feather. You don't want to attempt an elaborate, overly blocked performance because, taken out of the play's context, it may not read. Clarity and simplicity are the orders of the day. We're not dealing with through lines or relationships here. The basic acting rules do apply, of course (simple objectives, a sense of self-confidence, says Ed Hooks). But essentially you need a coach to help you shape your piece, not a scene-study teacher.

Warmups

Of course, you're going to be nervous when you arrive at the audition site. So what can you do about it? Mary Coleman, artistic associate in charge of casting at San Francisco's Magic Theatre, suggests finding a quiet place, perhaps trying a little yoga. Eric Maisel, author of *Performance Anxiety: What Everybody Should Know*, recommends a series of steps:

1. Read an audition book.

2. Think of auditioning not as an "art moment," but as a business moment.

3. Know who's auditioning you (they're people, not ogres).

4. Rehearse your entrance, not just your monologues (see next section).

5. Learn self-hypnosis, a trick that works for many musicians.

6. Concentrate on your breathing or try meditation.

7. Focus on stimuli around you, or use a "discharge" technique, like silent screaming, to get rid of pent-up emotion.

Moving, by the way, is better than standing still. Maisel doesn't shy away from mentioning prescription drugs for those who can't control the anxiety in other ways. Talk to your doctor about beta-blockers.

First Impressions

If all the directors we talked to emphasized any one thing, it was the importance of the first impression. From the first minute you enter the audition room, impressions are being formed. (Kelley says only half-jokingly that he forms impressions when he passes actors in their car on the freeway, walking in the parking lot, or standing in the bathroom.)

So here's the protocol: Enter the room when called. Have your resumé and photo in your hand (unless you've already given them to an assistant), not in the depths of your bag, and promptly hand it over. Smile pleasantly at the auditors and say "Hello," perhaps shake hands. Be prepared to chat if they show the inclination. Don't turn on an artificial hundred-watt smile. As Michael Addison, artistic director of the California Shakespeare Festival, says, "I'm not interested in surface charm. We're casting a rep company that's going to be together for seven months. I want to get to know the *person*."

Don't ask where to put your things; just put them down. Don't be deferential. Don't ask where to go and what to do (all that can be asked of the assistant before you enter the room). Take the stage calmly and confidently, about two-thirds of the way back if it's a proscenium stage. Introduce your piece(s)—name of play and character only—no synopsis, no description, not even if it's an original or obscure play (although if it is, you could mention the playwright). Your piece must stand on its own. Take a second or two, then begin.

Women often worry what to wear for an audition. The directors we talked to advised against the kind of revealing, sexy clothes some women don.

"Wear something loose and comfortable, like dressy rehearsal clothes," said one. "I need to be able to see what your body shape is like for costuming purposes, so don't wear anything too shapeless," cautioned another. "Don't wear a T-shirt with things written on it; it's distracting," said a third.

Addison points out that long skirts work well if you're auditioning for Shakespeare. Charles says that at a recent StrawHat audition in New York, more than half the women wore clothes that were just plain unflattering. "This is the last industry where we're allowed to ask to see a photo," she says. "The physicality of the person plays a large part. So why would you go to an audition not looking your best?"

Most of the directors agree that they decide within five to thirty seconds after a monologue begins whether they're interested in that actor, and that initial appearance and attitude is part of the decision.

Doing It

Don't look at the auditors when performing; it makes them feel responsible for your concentration. Choose a spot somewhere slightly above the auditors' heads. If you must talk to a chair, place it slightly downstage so you're still projecting out. Don't use an accent—auditors want to hear your natural voice; if you must use an accent, do it on only one of the two pieces you're doing—and then only if you're flawless. Don't be a talking head—move (many complaints from directors on this score). Don't rush. Speak loudly, but don't be too big for an audition situation. Don't mumble or comment to yourself or exclaim, "Whew!" when it's over—it makes you appear insecure.

And speaking of insecurity, what if you blow a line or blank out? Simply stop, apologize briefly, and take a breath. No harm done—although you certainly don't want to get a reputation for it. One director cautioned against going back over the same lines; she thinks you're sure to go up in the same spot. Simply jump ahead instead.

What's the bottom-line quality that directors look for, no matter the role to be cast? "Honesty." "The ability to really enjoy that moment of performance." "Focus, how much they're completely inside that piece, lit up like lanterns inside." "Believable humanity, full realization of every moment—no generalizing." "Make me laugh! I don't care if it's a gut-wrenching piece, you can still find one laugh."

One last word of advice: Don't be a victim. Maisel says, "You're giving a performance, not putting yourself on the line. Separate out what's about to happen from who you are."

As one actor says, "I tell myself I'm on a mission from God to help them."

11 | *When They're Calling You*

You've made the first cut. You were prepared and read your monologue or sang your song well enough so the director wants to see you again. You've gotten a place in the finals. You've been invited to the callbacks.

While still a part of the audition process, the callback is nevertheless significantly different from the first round of auditions. The director, presumably, now knows something about you—and likes that something. However, the director also knows something about everyone else invited back—and likes them, too. You're closer than you've been, but the competition is even tougher now.

How to Seal the Deal at Callbacks

Getting a part is like getting a job in any field. You submit an application and resumé. If you're lucky, you get an interview. And if you're very lucky, you get called back for a final interview.

Callbacks in the theater mean you are a finalist, too. As we pointed out in the introduction, if you make it this far, it's clear the director believes you have the potential to be a member of the cast. Here are some tips on how to realize that potential.

You want to be prepared to make the best impression possible. So be sure you understand what role or roles you're being considered for and what special preparation may be expected. Find out when you're expected to arrive, the type of reading you will be doing, and anything else you feel will help you do well. And, as we also pointed out, if you are being called back for a specific role, make sure you really want that role before accepting the invitation. A director appreciates your honesty. If you're not sure you're capable of handling the role, however, go anyway—the director believes you are.

It's important to understand what the director hopes to

get from the callback. Directors can structure callbacks in almost any way that makes sense to them, but, in general, callbacks allow them to do the following:

1. *Compare different combinations of actors for roles that interact.* Thus, if you're being considered for Hamlet's mother, you'll be reading with actors hoping to play both Hamlet and King Claudius. If you are up for the role of Dolly Levi, you may be reading with just about everyone.

2. *See how you take direction.* Good directors allow actors to experiment with different interpretations. They suggest a different reading or characterization and see how well you do with it. They look for signs that might indicate you are overly insecure, a poor listener, or just difficult to work with.

3. *Check for personality conflicts in the making.* See "The Seven Warning Signs of Auditions" in Chapter 23 and avoid *all* these behaviors.

4. *Listen to vocal quality* and see if you can change it, if necessary, to suit the director's idea of the character.

5. *Discover that indefinable something* that you bring to this role that no one else can.

6. *Check for conflicts* in the rehearsal and production schedule. Some actors believe that if they make it to callbacks, they are in a position to negotiate around other commitments. Most directors won't cast you if you will have to miss more than a few rehearsals. Some won't allow you to miss any.

Déjà Vu

You might assume that because you've been called back, you are a known quantity. Perhaps. But it's never safe to assume so. So, wear basically the same outfit you had on at auditions. Don't change your hairstyle or anything about the way you look. If a lot of people have auditioned, it's possible the director knows you as the person with the long red hair in the green turtleneck. If you show up wearing a blue T-shirt and your hair is now short and black, you've become an unknown quantity instead of someone they've looked forward to seeing again.

Similarly, for musicals, sing the same song or songs at the callback that you sang at the audition. They worked for you once and they'll work for you again. (If you are asked to sing something different, before you begin, simply remind them of what you sang the first time, and then proceed.)

If you audition frequently, keep a diary or a notebook (an appointment book is fine) in which you write down what you wore, for which parts you read, what you sang (if it was a musical), and for whom you auditioned. Find out the name of everyone who was there and who was interested in you. Those who like you may be able to offer you a role in another show in the future—or even now, since many people work on more than one project at a time. Keep a mailing list so from time to time you can let these people know you're still available.

Focus on Your Goal

Callbacks are more focused than auditions, so you need to be, too. In most cases, you'll be expected to know the show well. Always ask if scripts are available and what scenes will be read at callbacks. Read the entire script, not just the scenes you'll be asked to know. Do some reading about the play as well: the author, the period in which it was written (and the period in which it is set, if different), and critical commentary. Learn as much about your character as you can.

When you arrive for the callback, make sure you sign in, if necessary. There may be instructions or further information you'll need to know, as well as scripts or photocopied scenes to study.

Sit and listen attentively. Not only will you learn what works and what doesn't (pay close attention to the director's comments), but you'll see ways in which you can learn from the choices made by other actors, to use or set yourself apart from them. You also will indicate to the director and staff that you are a team player, someone who takes his or her work seriously.

When you're asked to read for the first time, it's reasonable to assume you can use the same interpretation you used at the audition, unless otherwise directed. However, you always can ask—and provide another opportunity to remind those evaluating you just who you are: "At auditions, I played Felix as prissy and a bit neurotic. Would you like me to do that again, or would you like more shading to his character?"

Because you'll be working with other actors, be friendly to everyone who attends callbacks. You never know with whom you'll be reading. (Or working. We know one actor who was not cast because she made a sarcastic comment about the audition space to someone who turned out to be the assistant director.) You'll do better if your

fellow actors are comfortable. Don't try to upstage or outshine anyone. You'll impress the director by your understanding of the role
and the play and by your attention to the art of ensemble playing.
(You can hone audition skills with classes in scene work or improvi-
sation, because both help you focus on the "now" and build observa-
tional, listening, and ensemble-playing skills.)

Into the Fray

There are ten essentials in reading a scene, which work equally well
in auditions and callbacks. In callbacks, however, these elements are
even more important because this is your final chance to show what
you can do.

1. *Relationship*. What is your relationship to the other character in
the scene? How does your character feel about him? Do you like or
dislike him? What do you want from him?

2. *Know What You're Fighting For*. You need to find a quick answer
to this, some sort of positive motivation that will propel you
through the reading. Conflict is the key because that is what creates
drama. We all want something. What does your character want?
What does the other character want? How do your desires conflict
with each other?

3. *Know What Just Happened*. The first lines of any scene begin in
the middle of some action. It's up to you to provide a sense of
what happened just before. You will stand out from other actors at
callbacks if you provide that sense. That's why it is so important to
know the entire play. When you read over the scene, consider
what you've been doing just before. It may be written or it may
not. In either case, you need to know—even if you have to make it
up yourself.

4. *Keep a Sense of Humor*. Yes, acting is serious business, and
getting the part is serious, too. But if you're too wrapped up in the
seriousness, you'll lose the sense of play. And this *is* a play.

5. *Play Opposites*. Play the gamut of motives and emotions, as
appropriate. Love and hate can coexist, just as can pride and
insecurity. Look for these opposites in any character you're reading
and use them.

6. *Go Beyond the Text*. While actors work from real life, there's
almost always more in the script than is obviously apparent. Some
of this can be deduced from a thorough reading of the script and

from critical commentary; some you may discover on your own. Whatever the source, use what you can to make your performance stand out, while still maintaining the author's intent.

7. *Communicate*. Acting is communicating—with an audience, a director, another actor. As many drama teachers point out, the two most common motives a character must communicate in a scene are: "I am right and you are wrong" and "Stop being who you are and become what I think you ought to be." Make these a part of your character and use the fact that these are part of the other characters as well.

8. *Heighten the Reality*. Plays wouldn't be very enjoyable if they dealt only with the day-to-day minutiae of existence. What a playwright does is distill reality into a series of important moments. Thus, you need to make the stakes in each scene as high as you can. Otherwise, why will anyone pay attention?

9. *Be Aware*. Actors like to talk about character and motivation, but less about what's going on—the *events* of the play. It might be a confrontation, a revelation, a turning point. But events have consequences and people are usually changed in some way. So ask yourself, "What happens in this scene? What are the changes—for my character and for others?" And then work toward those events and changes.

10. *Stay Grounded*. Auditions and callbacks are held on a bare stage or in a rehearsal hall—no sets, no costumes, no lights. It's up to you to create the reality of the play and your character. That means you have to visualize the actual location and what the characters are wearing. And you have to ground yourself in that reality so you can play it.

Working with the Director

If the director asks you to try something different, listen carefully. Make sure you understand precisely what he or she means. If you're not sure, paraphrase the request as a question: "In other words, you'd like me to play Franklin as slightly unhinged?" Remember, the director has something particular in mind, and there's no point in your proceeding unless you understand what that is. Occasionally, you'll get a less-than-specific direction: "Could you play Marie a little softer?" Before you proceed, make sure you know what is meant. Does the director mean with less volume? Or with less of an edge?

If you are asked for something different, make it *different*. You probably aren't going to be asked to repeat the scene, so go for a marked change, while still keeping to the director's suggestion. Thus, if you're asked to read Blanche Dubois, in her confrontation with Stanley Kowalski, with "more force," give it real force, not just more intensity. Get physical, scream, rant. The director can always pull you back, knowing all the while how far you can go if called for.

Occasionally, directors ask if anyone would like to read any other scene. In general, it's not a good idea to do so, unless you truly did badly the first time. Obviously, if everyone asked to read again, callbacks would last twice or three times as long as they do. However, if you feel you have a different interpretation you'd like to try—and the director offers additional time—go ahead. Just be aware this will be your final impression on those evaluating the actors. It may be better to leave well enough alone.

When the callbacks are finished, thank the director and staff. Make sure you know when you will be notified. The director or assistant usually announces this just before the callbacks are over. When you're told you can go, leave without lingering, unless you're asked to stay to provide additional information. Normally, the director and staff want to confer and can't do so until everyone has left. The decision-making has begun and you can only wait to learn the outcome.

When you get home, jot down in your notebook what you've learned: what things worked well and what didn't. What would you do the same and what would you do differently? What did you observe others do that you might use in the future? On which skills should you work?

Callbacks—like any other segment of the audition process—are about more than getting a part. They can and should be a learning experience.

12 | *Selling Yourself*

Auditioning is more than simply showing up; performing your monologue, cold reading, or song; and then waiting to see if your name is posted for callbacks. While ultimately your talent and appropriateness for the part—as shown by your performance during the audition—will determine your chances of getting cast, there are other things you can do to maximize those chances and get the most out of the audition. One of the most important is having an effective resumé that you can submit when you show up for your audition.

How to Put Together an Effective Resumé

JILL CHARLES

*I*f you want to work in theater, you'll need a theater resumé. And that's not the same as the resumé you might put together for other nontheatrical work. In general, the differences between a theater resumé and those you might be familiar with from other jobs reflect the freelance nature of theater work. A resumé in the "real world" usually starts with an "objective statement," then lists jobs held (working backwards from the most recent) in paragraph form, explaining the responsibilities for each position. In theater, this standard format would work for management positions—development, marketing, press relations, business manager—but not much else.

Directors, designers, stage managers, and technicians group their experience according to the particular area and position first, with dates secondary. Actors should not list dates at all, but rather list "best credit first." Finally, the job title for a standard position like "costume designer" or "master electrician" suffices for both an objective statement and an explanation of responsibilities performed in previous employment.

For any resumé to be effective, it should be laid out clearly with a pleasing sense of design. The wide availability of computers and laser printers makes it easy to use varying type sizes and fonts with boldfacing, italic type, or caps for emphasis and lines or boxes to separate sections. A good resumé is easy to read, not over-crowded, and presents the applicant in the most professional manner possible.

What follows is a general guideline to the currently accepted format for theatrical resumés. However, there are many different ways to format a resumé to get the necessary information on it, and each resumé should be constructed to best illuminate the experience and training of the individual. It is a good idea to look at others' resumés to get ideas for how to lay out your own. And if you can show yourself off to better advantage by creatively bending the rules a bit, go ahead—no one is going to report you to the resumé police.

Recognize that the printed page is only *half* of your total resumé package. The other half is your 8×10 photograph, attached to the back of your printed resumé (see Chapter 13). Therefore, your resumé must be limited to one page—in fact—to one 8×10 page rather than 8½ × 11. Anything else will mark you as a neophyte.

Here is the general outline of the actor's resumé, from the top down.

NAME

■ List only your professional name, if different from your legal name, in larger type than anything else on your resumé.

CONTACT INFORMATION AND PERSONAL STATISTICS

■ List unions, including Equity Membership Candidate or Eligible Performer status.

■ Give a phone number where you always will get the message.

■ If you are signed with an agent, list that office as your contact number.

■ Don't list your address, normally. If you're sending a resumé somewhere, the address will be on the cover letter. In some circumstances, you may want to write your address on the resumé, but it is safer in a resumé with a photo attached to leave off your address.

■ If you sing at all, list your voice (e.g., alto, baritone) and/or vocal range (some singers put their range in musical notation; others something like "Mezzo—belt to F#").

■ Indicate your citizenship and/or work-visa status, if you have credits from other countries or belong to Canadian or British Equity.

■ Include eye and hair color, height and weight (don't underestimate your weight by more than a few pounds—hopefully, they're going to see you in person, so they'll know).

■ Don't list clothing sizes on an acting resumé, although they should appear on modeling resumés.

■ Don't list your Social Security number; it's not needed until you're signing contracts.

■ Don't list your age unless you are under eighteen, in which case you *should* list your date of birth. Don't list an "age range"; let the casting people decide for themselves. (If you are asked at an audition how old you are, the proper response is, "How old is the character?")

CREDITS

■ Group credits under such headings as Theater, Film, and TV, or Regional and Stock Theater, New York Theater, Film and TV; use whatever headings make sense for your credits, and lead off with the section that contains your best credits.

■ List the play, the role, and where it was performed in columns across the page.

■ Identify the director as well, especially if he or she is well known in the profession.

■ Don't list the playwright unless it is a new play or reading.

■ In general, list professional credits above school credits, even if the professional role was smaller.

■ You also may use a single theater as a heading for a group of credits; for example, if you did five shows at one theater.

■ Don't list any dates! On an acting resumé, it's what you did, not when you did it, that matters. List in order of "best credit first" under each heading.

■ Indicate "understudy" or "u/s" or "u/s, performed once," as appropriate. However, if you actually took over for someone and performed a significant portion of the run, it's a legitimate credit without the "u/s" notation.

- Don't list scene studies or parts performed in acting class unless you really need to fill space.

- *Community* can be a pejorative label on a professional resumé; identify these credits with the name of the company or the theater building without specifying it was a community theater, if possible.

- Don't lie! There is always a fairly good chance someone looking at your resumé will have seen the production you claim you were in.

- Try to list credits that cover most genres and styles on your resumé (such as classical, musical, high comedy, contemporary, new plays). But don't overcrowd your resumé with everything you've ever done, unless you're new to the business and need to pad your resumé. Drop the lesser credits as you add new ones.

TRAINING

- List school(s), with degree(s), but not the year of graduation.

- Indicate the amount of specialized training, such as "Dance: ballet (6 yrs); jazz and tap (2 yrs)."

- List teachers if they are well known in their field, but don't clutter the resumé with the name of every person with whom you ever studied.

- Include internships or apprenticeships at professional theaters, at least while you're young and building up credits. List them here even though you also may have listed in your credits those roles you performed while an intern.

SPECIAL SKILLS

- This is your chance to communicate anything that makes you stand out in the crowd, and any skills that might prove useful for a commercial.

- List any related skills that may not be covered in your training section, such as dialects (specify which ones), musical instruments, stage combat, mime, and character voices.

- List sports, especially individual sports like diving or horseback riding, but don't go overboard. Indicating you are athletic and listing a few specialties is sufficient.

- Briefly list technical or management skills; in areas in which you have expertise, offer "resumé on request" (and have a copy of that resumé on hand at an audition).

■ Indicate if you have a license and can drive a car (standard and/or automatic) and/or a motorcycle.

■ Indicate if you have your own formal wear or period clothing, especially if you're interested in extra work.

■ "Good with children" or "good with animals" is fairly common, especially if you're interested in commercials.

■ Don't get overly cute, and be prepared to back up anything you list. If you say "squawk like a chicken," you'd better be able to do a convincing chicken at an audition.

Note one major difference from other theatrical resumés—no references. That's because your credits are identified by the producing theater and (usually) the director; these are your references. It is very common for one director who is considering using an actor to look down her resumé for a familiar name, and then call that director—or theater company—for a reference. It happens with such frequency, in fact, that you should be careful *not* to list any credits if you feel they would not give you a good reference for any reason. It's a good argument for not burning any bridges in this business—you could end up with a pretty short resumé.

Picture Perfect

13

Along with the resumé, a good headshot is essential for professional acting jobs or getting into an acting program—and very useful for almost any audition situation. Even for a small community theater, a quality headshot serves a purpose—it's a shorthand way for the director to remember you.

Making Sure Your Headshot Photo Is the Best It Can Be

Jill Charles

A cting is unique among all professions in our society today, in that a person's physical appearance is a legitimate consideration—even a deciding factor—for employment. For no other job is an applicant asked for a photo—in fact, in another arena, it would be illegal to request one.

But for the professional and aspiring professional actor, a photo is an essential tool for getting a job. Likewise, the photo is a necessary part of applications for many undergraduate and graduate theater programs, or for apprenticeships and internships in summer-stock and regional theaters. So even the preprofessional has need of a good "headshot."

Regardless of its immediate purpose—getting an audition or getting into a training program—your photo must do three things for you:

1. *Show Yourself As You Are.* One of the biggest mistakes of an inexperienced actor is to think the photo must be either "glamorous" or "theatrical." This misconception produces photos that won't look like you because you won't have a professional doing your makeup and styling your hair before

59

every audition. Even worse, these are photos that make you look cold and unapproachable.

2. *Pull the Viewers into the Shot, Intrigue Them, Make Them Want to See You in Person.* Because your eyes will go a long way in doing this, avoid photos that show so much of you—three-quarters or full body—that your eyes become insignificant in the overall picture. When your eyes "work" in a photo, they draw the viewer into it. Your personality comes through; at the same time, you leave the viewer with a sense there's a little mystery there—they'll have to see you in person to get the full effect.

3. *Present Yourself as a Professional.* This is why you use a professional photographer rather than a friend who is "good with a camera." Nor do you use your college yearbook picture, nor the one you had taken and framed for your mom's mantlepiece. This is also why you follow the current standards, arbitrary as they may be, because no matter for what purpose you use this photo, you will be in competition with others who have professional theatrical photos in that standard format.

Photo Styles

At the moment, there are two different "standard" types of photographs in use around the country, either of which is perfectly acceptable in any professional or preprofessional situation. The first is the headshot, which is an 8×10 enlargement of an actor's face, showing hair and neck, to or just below the collar. These are printed without a border on matte- or pearl-finish photographic paper. The actor's name is usually set in black type on a light area of the photo, or in white type on a dark area.

The second format is commonly referred to as a "three-quarters" or "portrait" shot, and shows the actor's head and shoulders at least, but may include down to the waist or lower—even as much as a full-body shot. These might be posed in many ways—seated, face leaning into one's hands; standing casually; perched on a stool; leaning against a wall—each one is unique.

These photos are printed showing the uneven black line that marks the edge of the photographer's negative frame, and then set within a wide white border. Again, the preferred paper is matte or pearl finish, with the name generally set in black inside the white border.

There is no need for an actor to choose one of these two types before going to a photographer. During the session, the photographer will allow for several changes of clothing and poses, and it is a simple matter of pulling the camera back a few feet to change a headshot into a portrait shot.

After looking at the contact sheet, the actor can select one (or several) of each type to have reproduced, and then decide which photo to send out on the basis of what seems most appropriate for the particular job. (Many commercial casting directors, for example, wish to see a headshot, while many directors prefer seeing more of an actor's body.)

Finding a Photographer

In the two largest entertainment markets, New York City and Los Angeles, there are literally hundreds of professional theatrical photographers. Smaller markets—Chicago, Seattle, Minneapolis, Boston, Philadelphia, San Francisco—may offer as few as one or as many as a dozen photographers who specialize in photographing entertainers.

While there is a generally accepted format for the theatrical photo, within each of these markets there may be very subtle variations—largely because a very few photographers handle entertainment professionals and have left their own personal stamp on most of the photos in that market. So the best advice for any actor living in or moving to one of those markets is to have photos done in that city, by whichever professional theatrical photographer your research indicates will do the best job for you.

Many actors and aspiring students, however, live where there is no direct access to such professionals and as such need to create a theatrical photo taken by a professional photographer—which is a slightly different process than having a photo taken by a professional theatrical photographer. This is not an impossible challenge, but it does necessitate that you know exactly what is needed and have the confidence to firmly guide the photographer into that mode.

Remember that in selecting a photographer, you are not looking for the "best" photographer, but rather for the one with whom you can work well to achieve the best photograph of yourself. The most expensive, best-known theatrical photographer in New York may not be the right choice for you if you are intimidated by the reputation or feel no rapport with him or her. A superb wedding photographer may not be flexible enough to do a much less formal shot of an actor or, indeed, to work with black-and-white film.

Any professional photographer will have a portfolio for you to look through, and there are clues to be seen there, whatever the subject matter. Do the subjects look different from each other? Do they invite you into the frame with their eyes, so that you want to learn more about them?

Notice the technical facility of the photographer: Are skin tones (that is, textures) realistic? Does lighting show features clearly, neither washing out portions of the face nor hiding any area in shadow? Can you tell which subjects in a black-and-white photo are blondes (the hardest hair color to light)? When talking to photographers who do not normally do theater shots, show them some examples and ask if they are comfortable with the style.

Ask for complete details about fees, number of shots, guarantees, retouching, and makeup artist. Most photographers will tell you they keep the negative as their own property. That's all right; you need only one positive print of each picture that you choose (probably between two and four altogether), which you will have retouched and then reproduced.

Clothing and Makeup

The best clothing choices for a general shot are casual—a shirt and sweater or perhaps a vest or jacket over a shirt or tank top. If you are marketable as an executive type for commercials and industrials, then you probably also would bring along a suit for some of the session. Colors will read only as intensity, and it's best to avoid stark black or white. Choose a color that will translate to the shade of gray that will offer a natural contrast to your skin color. Some patterns are acceptable if not so bold as to be distracting and if the contrast in the pattern is not too bright.

Plaids and subtle stripes usually work quite well, as do textured sweaters, denim, and rough weaves. Hats and props are generally unnecessary and "cutesy," although if you usually wear glasses, you should do some of your photos wearing them. If you're really unsure about clothing selection, have a friend take a roll of black-and-white Polaroids of you in various outfits to help you decide.

Should you do your own makeup or pay for a professional? If you feel completely competent and at ease with your own makeup, then you may choose to do it yourself. However, it's essential to remember that you are making up for black-and-white film, so color is seen as shadow. This means cheek color should go lower to accent the cheekbone; if it is applied on the cheekbone (as you would in your normal daytime makeup, to add color) it will take out the contour. Eye shadow works the same way; it will not read as color, but will deepen your eye sockets. Eyeliner should be soft, applied sparingly with a brush, with very little on the lower lid; apply mascara as you would normally. Lipstick is another example of color being meaningless—it is the contrast to your skin, not the color, that will show.

Men might want to use a little bit of cream base to lighten a very heavy beard, as photos tend to accent dark beards. An actor who frequently wears a beard might want to get the most out of a session by doing a full range of facial hair—first shooting with full beard and mustache, then shaving to mustache only, then clean-shaven.

Shave carefully and, if you have had a beard for a long time, be prepared to add makeup to even out the tones of your face. The look of a few day's growth of beard was popular for a few years, but seems to have waned. However, if you feel it's right for your "type" and could improve casting potential in some situations, you can try some shots with a rough look, then shave for the remainder.

At the Photo Session

It is essential to create an action at the photo shoot, so the finished photo is a moment captured in active time, not a pose. Theatrical shots always should be with the eyes playing directly to the camera lens.

Consider this as an acting assignment. Imagine the camera lens is a specific person you care about, and then invite that person to join you in some action. For instance, the camera becomes a close friend you haven't seen for a long time. Take yourself through the actions of seeing and recognizing the friend, feeling a quick jump of joy at the surprise meeting, and then planning something fun you can share together. Meantime, while you are concentrating on this acting exercise, the camera is snapping away, capturing real moments in time, not frozen facial poses.

To achieve an active, natural smile with your eyes as well as your mouth, try creating a situation where you are sharing something with a child, or calling a child to come to you so you can show them something very special. Say a sentence out loud: An enthusiastic "Come with me!" can help present a bright expression, and the word *me* shows teeth.

Selecting, Retouching, Reproducing

It will help to look at your contact sheets with a loupe (a magnifier) and a sheet of white paper with a square the size of one picture cut out of it. Show the contact sheets to a few trusted friends in the business, including a director or casting director, if you can.

When you have selected your photos and had them printed by the photographer as 8×10s, have them retouched to soften lines a bit, perhaps lighten darkness under the eyes, and to remove blemishes that are not permanent. Most photographers don't have a retoucher in their studio, but can usually recommend somebody; or retouching can be done in the reproduction lab.

It is tempting, but generally not wise, to use photographic means—either lighting or retouching—to disguise or hide physical traits like crooked teeth, birthmarks, your weight, or the shape of your nose. This can backfire if a busy casting person calls you in on the basis of what was seen in a photo, and that's not what he or she sees when you come in the door.

Your final step is to have the original prints, now retouched, reproduced in quantity. (This would cost a fortune if you had the photographer do it; fortunately, reproduction labs make prints in quantity very inexpensively.)

It is important that the original print you get from the photographer be in correct contrast: black hair should have detail in it; very light skin should have texture. Reproductions generally increase the contrast (light goes lighter, dark goes darker), so the original print needs to be as sharp as possible.

The reproduction process involves rephotographing your original 8×10 to produce a large negative, or *interneg*, which then is used to make the inexpensive copies. Before the copies are run off from this negative, most labs offer a test print for a little extra cost. This is highly recommended, especially if you are sending your photo away to a reproduction house in another city.

When inspecting the test print, look for the closest possible similarity to the original print in terms of contrast and skin tone. The poor reproduction of your photograph can destroy the uniqueness you and your photographer worked so hard to achieve.

If you are having your name applied to the photo, this will be done to the original, before the copy negative is shot.

Lithography is a much cheaper method of reproduction, although these prints lose much of the depth of a real photograph. You may decide to have a smaller quantity done by the more expensive photographic method and then a larger quantity of lithographs. That way, you could do a general mailing to hundreds of regional theaters, for example, using the lithographs, while saving the "good" photos for handing out at auditions.

Never underestimate the importance of a good photograph—one that looks like you and that you feel proud to hand to a casting director. The process of having your photo made represents a significant investment, and it is one worth doing well the first time—handing out a bad photo is just an expensive means of putting your acting goals on hold.

14 | *Actors: Did You Know?*

*T*he "Did You Know?" department has been a prominent feature of *Stage Directions* since the magazine's very first issue in 1988. Short items about sundry theatrical subjects gleaned from companies across America, various readings, conversations, and other sources, "Did You Know?" offers an assortment of perspectives. Here are some hints and pieces of advice on auditions culled from ten years of "Did You Know?"

Do It Again

"When you get a callback, try to do the same exact thing you did in the original audition," advises Doug Moston in *Coming to Terms with Acting* (Drama Books). "That is why you're being called back. Resist the temptation to 'make it better.' Making it better means you're changing it. Be careful." Moston also suggests wearing the same clothes you wore at the first audition, since that will help the director remember you.

Come in from the Cold

When attempting a cold reading at an audition, expect that you may fluff a line or two, and don't apologize. Directors know mistakes will be made. Instead, concentrate on the next line to be read. Don't go back and correct yourself either. You spoil whatever momentum or character you've created. Imagine how painful it must be for directors to witness an actor's obvious distress. Don't aid in making them uncomfortable—you want to create a positive feeling about your work.

Find the Meaning

When reading for a part for which you cannot find proper motivation, consider using the desire to change your partner. The change desired must be concrete in your mind—for example, "I love you, but if you'd only. . . ."

At First Sight

Sight-reading is a skill normally linked to musicians, but actors need to be able to read a script aloud—and confidently—at auditions and rehearsals. As Hugh Morrison points out in his book *Acting Skills* (Routledge), a good sight-reader is quick to comprehend the meanings and nuances of a text. When asked to read, the actor must have time to look over the script, develop a short strategy, and make an intelligent guess at the meaning of the text and the viewpoint of the character. But from where does such a skill come? From practice. Reading plays aloud with friends is an excellent way to develop this skill. Perhaps you or your theater company might want to start a play-reading group. It's not only a good way to develop sight-reading and other vocal skills, but also a good way to audition plays for possible production.

Monologue Source

An excellent source of monologues is Edgar Lee Masters' *Spoon River Anthology*. This book of poems, first published in 1915, is a series of "epitaphs," the story of each dead person's life and most often how they came to die. Some are dramatic, some comic, some matter of fact. They can be used individually or with the introduction, as a group. One person can do several to show his or her dramatic range, or they can be done separately if short pieces are needed, as in a class. Because the poems are in free verse, they are easy to speak. And because they cover the full range of human emotion, you can pick out those that best suit a particular person or performance need.

The Best Defense . . .

When an actor upstages you in an audition reading, use it. Register your awareness—with humor—of the situation; then be willing to compete. If the actor invents some bit of business or an imaginary prop, acknowledge it and work with it. Otherwise, all attention will be diverted from your performance.

Getting Past It

In an audition, writes Michael Shurtleff in *Audition* (Walker & Co.), don't stop if you're doing badly. Instead, get angry at your reading partner or kiss your partner and offer words of endearment. "Either way—even if it doesn't jibe with the script—will connect you with your partner, will create a relationship, will renew what you're fighting for, and will interest the auditors in you. There's nothing to be gained by stopping and everything to be gained if you take a big blame-or-love risk to rescue yourself."

Tips from an Expert

Acting coach Ed Hooks says he gets calls from actors who feel that if they don't put their entire lives at the disposal of the director, he or she won't cast them. "But you have to have a life," says Hooks, "and any director who would not cast you because you insist on a realistic time commitment probably didn't want you that much in the first place." He recommends being proactive: Work with the director to set up a reasonable rehearsal schedule. His other piece of advice seems like common sense, but he says you'd be surprised how many naive actors are out there. "Never go to an audition at someone's home if that person is a stranger. And it goes without saying," adds Hooks, "never take your clothes off at an auditioner's request."

Auditions and Directors | 15

Organization is the director's best friend. If the audition is planned well, there will be more time to make good decisions. The audition itself will go more smoothly and you are much more likely to be pleased with the cast you have chosen. Good decisions generally mean good casting.

Organization takes planning, and planning takes many forms, beginning with extensive analysis of the play and characters. That will pay off in the audition process itself. For an overview of the planning, preparation, and running of auditions, see "Casting a Wide Net," Chapter 16.

You can't cast the right people if they don't show up at your auditions. So if you want to get the right people to auditions, your planning must include thinking about the audition announcement. You need to spell out what you expect. A good audition announcement does more than give time and location and the name of the play. (See "Let Them Know What You Want," Chapter 18.)

Where will you hold auditions? Directors do not always have a choice of audition space. However, if alternatives exist, you may want to consider two possibilities. One approach is to hold the auditions in a space that approximates the actual size of the stage. In fact, many directors use the stage itself. Others, however, prefer to audition actors in a more intimate environment, where they can get a good look at the people and start forming a relationship from the start. When you're in the auditorium and forced to call up to the stage, there is such a distance between you and the performers. On the other hand, many directors like to see the actors as the audience will see them. However, novice actors often are more nervous on a stage than they would be in a rehearsal hall.

Many directors prefer that actors not read from the script at auditions. One reason is that it becomes increasingly tiresome to hear the script again and again. Another, and perhaps more important reason, is that a director won't be influenced by faulty interpretation of the script. If you are listening for the "right" approach from actors who don't know what you really want, you may miss out on talent that dares to be different. Whether you use the script or use other material, make sure you have enough copies on hand, clearly marked so people can find them easily. You might want to make copies available ahead of time so people can work with them.

Outline beforehand how you want to use the audition time frame. Unless you require that everyone show up at the same time, you're likely to have people drop in over the entire period. One way to handle this is to set cycles of readings, so newcomers can be worked in. Make sure your actors understand how the audition will be structured. A handout given to all those present is the best way to make certain everyone understands. The handout also can include the basic information you offered in the announcement (dates, character breakdown, director's intentions). Even if people have read this before (and not everyone does), they may not remember. More important, it gives actors something on which to focus and emphasizes once again what the show is about.

While some directors don't mind actors delivering lines to them directly, others find this distracting. If you are among the latter, just stop the audition and kindly explain. Or write it down on a short list of suggestions that you pass out ahead of time.

It's essential to take good notes during auditions. An audition form on which you can write makes things easy. Develop a set of symbols that only you know, a kind of shorthand that you can use to rate the performers. For example: O (Outstanding, should be cast); V (Very good, possible); A (Adequate, usable sometime); N (Not adequate); U (see "The Seven Warning Signs of Auditions," Chapter 23).

Symbols allow you to write notes with some degree of assurance that you can be honest without hurting anyone's feelings should that person see your comments.

How you run auditions is in great part related to the show you're casting, your pool of talent, the amount of time you have for evaluations, and your directorial style. You'll find several different approaches in the articles "Audition the Actor, Not the Part" (Chapter 22), as well as "Casting a Wide Net" (Chapter 16). Special consideration is given to auditioning youngsters in "Children Will Listen" (Chapter 24) and actors with disabilities in "Everyone Onstage" (Chapter 26). You'll also find advice on double-casting in "Double, Double . . ." (Chapter 25), and things to watch for (good and bad) in "Eight Things to Look for in Auditions" (Chapter 21) and "The Seven Warning Signs of Auditions" (Chapter 23).

You can structure callbacks in almost any way that makes sense to you. Just be sure everyone else understands what you intend to do. That structure depends on how well the auditions went, but in general callbacks allow you to:

■ Compare two or more actors for the same role.

■ Compare different combinations of actors for roles that interact (for example, parent and child, man and wife, boss and employee, king and queen, policeman and thief).

■ See how actors take direction. This is crucial. Take time to allow actors to experiment with different interpretations. Suggest a different reading or characterization and see how well they do with it. Look for signs that might indicate an unwillingness to compromise.

■ Watch for personality conflicts in the making (see Chapter 23).

■ Listen to vocal quality and see if the actor can change it, if necessary, to suit your idea of the character.

■ Check for a blend of physical and emotional characteristics. Few plays feature clones. For the sake of the play and the sake of the audience, try to cast a wide spectrum of physical and emotional types.

■ Check for conflicts in the rehearsal and production schedule. Some actors believe if they make it to callbacks, they are in a position to negotiate around other commitments. You'll have to decide now whether casting a particular actor is worth the aggravation of missed rehearsals.

Once you've made your choices, you'll need to contact the actors. See "The Moment of Truth," Chapter 27.

Finally, when it's all over, jot down notes of what went well and what didn't. You may think you'll remember all this the next time around, but once you're into rehearsal, your mind will have moved on to other things. Consider not only the audition process, but also the preparation, location, and all other factors.

Casting a Wide Net | *16*

Here's an overview of the entire audition process from the director's perspective—from early preparation to callbacks and beyond.

Choosing the Right Actor for the Role Is Essential—Here's How to Do It

JILL CHARLES

*P*roper casting is critical to a good production. Good casting will mean rehearsals move smoothly and quickly along to the critical element—interpreting the play. Conversely, poor casting can mean getting bogged down in individual coaching, compensating for something that will never be absolutely right—trying to fit a round peg into a square hole. To put it even more bluntly, good casting can hide a play's weaknesses, while bad casting can destroy even the "bulletproof" show. Here's some advice on how to make the most of your casting opportunities.

Do Your Homework

Good casting begins with extensive homework, before the director even arrives at the first audition. After the play has been selected, reread it several times, making notes on each character from these three perspectives:

1. *What are the character's essentials, as dictated by the play, in terms of physical type, age, gender, ethnicity, and so on?* This aspect has broadened considerably over the last decade, with

nontraditional casting finding favor and wide acceptance. Directors working with a pool where women outnumber men, for instance, may find that many male roles can be played by women without disturbing the play. (Note, however, that some playwrights forbid such changes, as clearly stated in the royalty contract.) But there are still requirements within each play that the director must heed to make the play work. For instance, casting a conventionally beautiful woman as Lizzie in *The Rainmaker* undermines the heart of the play, unless makeup and hairstyle can alter her looks.

2. *How do you see the character, physically and emotionally?* While it is counterproductive to walk into auditions with a conviction that "Blanche must be blonde," you still need to be familiar with your own preconceptions of the character, those that come unbidden while reading the play. Recognizing and examining those first instincts actually helps you jettison them if a surprise comes along in auditions that is an improvement on what you originally had imagined.

3. *What is the bottom line for the audience regarding each character? For whom should they be rooting? Which two people will they want to end up together?* Finding an actor to play Garfinkle in *Other People's Money*, for example, is a challenge because the audience must believe this man is the heartless shark everyone calls him—yet, must like him in spite of it and be glad he winds up with Kate in the end. A director who casts a "brilliant" actor without charisma as Garfinkle will be fighting a losing battle.

Running the Audition

The way an audition is run will vary greatly from one type of production to another. Professional auditions are individual readings, as required by Actors Equity, although there may be a prior general audition where actors present monologues. In general, from ten to thirty actors per role—pulled from files or from submissions by actors themselves and/or agents—are scheduled for auditions by the casting director. You'll find this type of audition at many semiprofessional and community theaters as well, though readings may be open to all who sign up.

What's most important about running the individual-reading audition is to keep it efficient and on schedule. Don't overbook audition times. A good rule of thumb for readings is to schedule eight actors per hour, at ten-minute intervals, with two extra actors scheduled in at fifteen and forty-five minutes after the hour: 10:00, 10:10, 10:15,

10:20, 10:30, 10:40, 10:45, 10:50. This will only work, however, if you know that an individual audition will not run more than seven minutes on average.

Generally, in a professional audition situation, a reader is used rather than having actors read scenes with each other. The advantage to this method is that the director focuses all attention on one actor. The reader should be familiar with the scene and read it intelligently, but without trying to act it.

As a rule, keep the scene for this first audition short (generally, one to two pages). List two scenes but inform the actors they probably will read only one. This way, when you see immediately that an actor is not what you are looking for, you can be finished after a three-minute reading and move on to the next person. This way you will stay on or ahead of schedule, so when an exciting actor comes along, you'll have time to read the second scene.

Keeping the atmosphere friendly and courteous is important. Take the time for a brief conversation—acknowledging how you know the actor's work or commenting on her resumé—to help personalize this artificial situation. When ready to begin, introduce the reader, saying, "Jack will be reading with you, starting where it's marked on page 23. Whenever you're ready."

Come up with a good tag line that lets the actor know the audition is over, but is not dismissive: "Thank you so much for showing us your work today. We'll be deciding about callbacks later in the week." This will let the actor know tactfully that if he hasn't heard from you by the end of the week, he's not in the running.

Group Readings

An audition method that can be particularly effective in academic and community theaters is to have all those auditioning (up to as many as twenty at a time) sit on the stage in a semicircle, facing the director who is out in the house. If you expect a large number of people at auditions, have them sign up for a full-hour time slot, in groups of twelve. The audition scenes should be posted well in advance and assignments made beforehand as to which actors will read which parts and in which order. As pairs or small groups of actors are called upon to read a scene, they step forward into the semicircle and play it to the director, then return to their seats.

Explain to those auditioning that every actor may not read for every part in which they are interested, but they will be considered for all roles (unless they specifically ask not to be), and may be called back for a role that they didn't read at the first round of auditions.

At first, there may be some resistance to this technique, but there are many advantages for the director. If it is a group you don't know very well, you have their faces in front of you at all times. You can make a chart of the actors' names, from left to right, and keep it in view. This method allows you to make constant physical comparisons, looking at different combinations of people as you read them, mixing and matching if need be. In most amateur situations, this is preferable to doing individual auditions and then wondering how the woman you're auditioning at 8:30 A.M. would look with that man who came in at 7:45 P.M.

Although actors at first may feel highly competitive in this mode, there is an element of competition in any audition; actually, this arrangement more quickly dispels such feelings than other methods. The actors who step forward are "supported" by the physical arrangement of those sitting in the circle, and this usually becomes an emotional support as well. Meanwhile, those seated are watching other actors' auditions, and this often will help student actors understand and accept, in retrospect, why they may not have been cast as they wished.

Callbacks

Call back only the actors in whom you are seriously interested, probably from two to six per role. Calling back actors you know you would never cast is a waste of everyone's time; however, it is wise to have a few backups in mind, in case the actor you want turns down the role or must leave the show at some point. Make use of your "homework" to select scenes for callbacks that are key to the character: the wittiest dialogue for a comedy, or one of the more emotionally demanding scenes (though not necessarily the climax of the play) for a drama. At this point, you may choose to pair up actors to read scenes together rather than using a reader; if that is done, however, it is essential that each actor feels that he or she is given equal attention.

Allow ten to fifteen minutes for each callback and take the time to talk with the actors you don't know, to get a sense of how you would work together. Trust your instincts if you sense a difficult attitude; a brilliant but "high-maintenance" actor frequently is just not worth the effort needed to keep him happy, nor the toll he takes on the company's morale. In callbacks, it is an excellent idea to let actors read a scene, then ask for an adjustment of some kind, and have them repeat a page of the scene with that adjustment. This will show you how quickly and well they take direction or, conversely, how "married" they are to their own interpretation.

Making Tradeoffs

Casting is largely about compromise. It is rare that a director comes out of auditions on any level—professional, community, academic—absolutely ecstatic about every single cast member. There are no hard and fast rules here; every situation is different. Probably the two most common dilemmas are deciding between instinct and experience, and between type and talent.

For example: Two actors audition for a comic role, and one seems to be a genuinely funny human being, but has minimal credits on his resumé compared to the other. In this instance, you must decide how great a risk you are willing to take on instinct over experience. A natural comic instinct is a rare attribute and can compensate for many other things, including lack of experience. In this situation, you would have to take into account the length of the part, the length of rehearsal time, and how long and hard you are willing to work to overcome this actor's lack of experience. In a summer-stock situation with a ten-day rehearsal period, you might cast this role with the more experienced actor, but cast the natural comedian in a college production with six weeks of rehearsal.

An agonizing decision directors must often make is whether to use a less talented actor who is absolutely the right age and type for a role or to push the character's credibility with the audience by casting a more talented actor who is less appropriate for the part.

For instance, suppose a thirty-five-year-old actress is clearly the more capable performer, but the less talented twenty-year-old is completely believable as the college student indicated in the part. Consider the context: Would the older actress be surrounded by other twenty-year-olds as "classmates" or can you raise the age of all the "young" parts and make the contrast less obvious? Are you stuck with a thirty-six-year-old actor playing her father, or do you have a fifty-five-year-old actor you can cast in that role?

In general, it's best to go with the stronger talent and let the audience stretch its suspension of disbelief. However, there is a point at which, if the actor is simply unbelievable as the character, you lose the audience altogether. If you find yourself on the horns of such a dilemma, you might bring in another person with an objective eye to tell you if they can "buy" that actor as the character. A more extreme solution might be to extend auditions further, and look for a third actor who has the talent *and* the look.

The Cast List

If at all possible, sleep on your decisions before posting them and until then, resist the temptation to give any actor any indication of whether he or she is cast or in what role. Breaking this rule often leads to extremely uncomfortable situations, much worse than letting the actors worry for one night whether they were cast.

If actors come to you afterwards with questions, be as honest as possible about your casting decisions, always explaining that casting is based on many circumstances besides "talent." And just as an actor must accept the casting and get on with it, a director must do the same—no point in continuing to agonize over choices you made or wish that your favorite for the lead hadn't pulled out before callbacks. Get on with rehearsals; make it work with what you have. I have found that an actor who was a second or even third choice at auditions invariably proves so wonderful in the role that, by opening, I couldn't imagine anyone else doing the part.

Good Auditions Need Good Publicity

17

Tips to Get the Word Out—and Actors In

A casting notice or audition announcement should be as detailed as you can make it. First, you want performers to be fully prepared so the audition can move along smoothly and efficiently. Second, you're more likely to get the people you need if you make it clear just what you're looking for.

The most complete casting notice should be in your company newsletter or in a flyer mailed to members, local schools, and other theater companies. Newspapers usually won't print lengthy notices; instead, give a summary of what you need and a contact name and phone number. Some answering machines accept one- or three-minute outgoing message cassettes onto which you can record a great deal of information. Be sure to allow for callers to leave a message in case they have a question.

To be truly complete, a casting notice should contain the following ten elements:

■ *The name or working title of the production and the producing company.* Include the name of the director or person in charge of the actual audition and a message phone number to contact for more information.

■ *A brief description of the production and how it will be presented* (for example, in the round, dinner theater, or outdoors). A one-line description of the play is helpful, especially if it's an original or not well known.

■ *A list of characters*, even if you think "everybody" knows the play and you are casting it traditionally. Be as specific as possible: include gender, age range, and character type.

■ *If appropriate, specify height, hair color, or ethnicity*. If the character sings, give the vocal range; if the character dances, tell what kind of dancing is required. If you are going to cast a role or roles in a nontraditional manner, say so.

■ *An explanation of how you want the performers to prepare*. Should they be ready with a monologue or a scene with a partner? From a classic or modern play? From a comedy or drama? Or will you conduct cold readings? Will they be required to sing? If so, is accompaniment provided? What kind of song should they sing? Should it be from the show? What's needed from dancers? Is there any special dress requirement?

■ *The name and address of the audition location*. Give *specific* directions if it's hard to find.

■ *Where rehearsals will be held and for how long*; people may need to look over their calendars. Also, tell where and when the actual production will take place and the length of the run.

■ *If you want to do some prescreening, give a phone number and make sure there is someone—or an answering machine—ready to take the calls*. Prescreening gives you the chance to chat with unfamiliar applicants and determine their potential. It also helps them come to the audition better prepared.

■ *If there could be some doubt, state clearly whether pay is involved*. You don't have to say how much. If you're working under a union contract, say which union and contract. Also note whether you're looking for union performers only or for both union and non-union.

■ *Some audition notices include a note from the director, explaining his or her enthusiasm and personal vision of the show*. If you've got room, this can add a human face to what many people see as the worst experience in life short of death by fire.

Let Them Know What You Want | *18*

An Audition Announcement—and Packet—Makes Things Go More Smoothly

A good audition serves the common interest of both director and actor. Both want the auditions to go smoothly. The director wants to cast the show and the actors want to be cast. The director wants the actors to do their best and so do they.

So, as a director, how do you get the right people to audition and to audition well? Aside from issues over which you have no control (the pool of acting talent in your area, for example), the simplest answer is to provide all the information the actors need to prepare and perform well, and to understand the commitment they must make to the show.

Audition announcements are standard operating procedure. However, in too many cases, the announcements are bare-bones at least. If you want to get the right people to auditions, you need to spell out what you expect. A good audition announcement does more than give time and location and the name of the play. Indeed, the more information you can share with those auditioning, the better. On the other hand, you don't want to overwhelm people. Perhaps the best way is to present a brief outline of essential audition information in the announcement, and then make available a more complete set of information in the form of an audition packet, available before or during auditions.

The Announcement

The announcement itself should have the following: name of production, playwright name, name of director, production dates, audition dates and times, list of characters (including gender and age), and a brief description of the audition setup (for example, cold or prepared readings and whether scripts are available). Make sure there is a contact name and phone number, as well as the address of the rehearsal location, and a place or contact for the audition packet.

The Packet

Because the audition announcement is widely distributed, it is normally on one sheet of paper, keeping the cost down. However, for those who want to know more about the play and the production envisioned by the director, an audition packet contains all this information, but in significantly greater detail. Let's take a look at the packet, which may contain four to eight or more pages of information.

TIME COMMITMENT

Make sure you include when rehearsal starts and what days and times, and complete production dates and times (don't forget to include pickup rehearsals, if you plan to have them). This will give actors a chance to see if they have time conflicts.

THE PLAY ITSELF

Begin with a synopsis of the play, particularly if it's not well known. A few sentences on the author are helpful—as are comments on the play's literary, social, or historical importance—and any awards or critical acclaim it may have received.

CHARACTER BREAKDOWN

List all the characters, including name, age, physical and emotional characteristics, relationship to other characters, and special requirements if needed (*an ability to leap onto a tall something, for example*).

THE DIRECTOR'S VISION

To be familiar with a play is helpful to the actor, but so is the vision the director brings to this particular production. You might explain why you want to do this show, what attracts you about it. Also take time to give a sense of the particular style or approach you intend to use.

THE AUDITION PROCESS

Make it clear whether you intend to use cold readings, or prepare a reading or monologue in advance. Be as explicit as possible. Actors will appreciate it, and you'll have to answer fewer questions during the audition. In addition to giving the time and place of the audition, you might suggest that everyone arrive at the beginning to hear what others are doing, or to allow you to start grouping people in readings immediately. If the audition is by appointment only, make it clear how long before the appointed time the actors may arrive and where they should wait. Put yourself in the actors' place and consider all the questions they might have. Then answer them.

SCRIPTS OR SCENES

Making scripts (or selected scenes) available beforehand is beneficial to the actors and to an efficient audition process. Cold readings are not always avoidable, but they almost always are less satisfactory for both actor and director than a prepared audition. If you don't want (or can't afford) to make multiple copies available, ask if your local library will put several on reserve—available to check out for a limited time. (In the following example from North Carolina's Theatre Charlotte, scripts can be checked out from the theater with a $25 security deposit). Or provide (or create) your own monologues from the script, one for each character.

A LITTLE HISTORY

A brief explanation of your theater company helps place the production in perspective. While many people may have worked with you before, not everyone will have an understanding of your company's history; even those who have may not really know as much as you think they do. Mention how long you've been around, some of the shows you've done, awards you've won. A few paragraphs will do the job. (This is a good place to underscore basic virtues like respect, cooperation, and teamwork.)

The entire packet should be printed double-sided (saves paper) and stapled at the top left corner. This keeps everything together. If you have an audition form that customarily is filled out at the audition itself, you might consider including that in the packet. That way, people already have done this work before they arrive. The packet also should contain all pertinent contact information, in case someone has a question or concern that needs to be addressed before the audition.

Put it all together. You'll find the actors will be more "together" as well.

Casting Call

Here's an effective audition announcement for the Theatre Charlotte production of *Follies*:

> *Follies* is a haunting memory piece that takes place on the stage of a decaying old theater, to which a number of retired *Follies* performers have been invited for a final reunion before the theater is demolished. A ghostly aura surrounds these grand old ladies and gents as they revive their glittery old routines while rekindling friendship, rivalry, romance, and betrayal.
>
> Filled with memory, illusions, and disillusions of love, this lavish musical weaves lyrics, music, costumes, and choreography into an elegant tapestry of theater nostalgia.
>
> The winner of seven Tony Awards, *Follies* features a sophisticated and penetrating score by Stephen Sondheim. In addition to director Keith Martin and Designer Vernon Carroll, *Follies* will feature guest artists John Coffey as musical director and Ron Chisholm (who appeared in the national tour of *Follies*) as choreographer. Roles are available for 23 men and 25 women from teenage through 70. The pre-audition workshop will be held at 7:30 P.M. on Monday, July 10. Auditions will be held at 7:30 P.M. on Monday and Tuesday, July 24 and 25. Scripts are available for overnight checkout; a $25 deposit is required.
>
> Performance dates are September 14 through October 1.

A Good Form Can Make Auditions Easier | 19

Make It Easy on the Actors and Yourself

A good audition form, like the one shown on p. 86, should be explicit in what information is needed and simple to fill out. Too many of those we have seen are neither, mostly because the needs of the director and those of the actors haven't been considered. Many actors at auditions will be nervous and distracted; for this reason alone, the form should be easy to read (ours is shown about 50 percent of actual size) and fill out.

Beware of clutter. The form should look organized and ask information in an obvious sequence. If you don't make the sequence clear, actors inadvertently may skip over a section. The form shown here solves that problem with four sections, each clearly numbered: Personal Data, Audition Information, Agreement [contract], and Skill Summary. A fifth section is set aside for director's comments during the audition.

You can ensure that the actor provides you with enough information by having a separate box for each item. Note that under Personal Data, there are separate boxes for name, date, address, city, zip, home and work phones, and vocal range (if applicable). An empty box shouts, "Write in me."

Of course, you can't get pertinent information if you don't ask for it. What's pertinent? Try to ask only what you need for the purposes of the audition and for contacting

---

The Poorhouse Players	**Audition Form**

1. Personal Data

Your name		Today's date
Address	City	Zip
Home phone	Work/Message phone	Vocal range

2. Audition Information

Role(s) auditioning for:

If not cast in the above role(s) will you accept another? ❏ Yes ❏ No	Will you perform in the ensemble (if any)? ❏ Yes ❏ No

Will attending rehearsals create problems for you in terms of time, money, transportation or energy? ❏ Yes ❏ No

Consider your time commitments. Try to list all the expected things that might keep you from rehearsals. This information will be used in scheduling, so try to be as complete as possible.

3. Agreement

I understand that if I am cast in this production I will not participate in any other theatrical production for six weeks prior to opening night. I understand that exceptions will be made only with the approval of the director .

Sign here _____

4. Skill Summary

Cast members are expected to put in at least four hours of non-performing work—two hours in either set or costume construction and another two hours to be determined by the volunteer coordinator. Please check your preferences:

Set construction ❏ building ❏ painting ❏ decorating
OR
Costume construction ❏ sewing ❏ non-sewing
AND
❏ Publicity ❏ Set Moving ❏ House ❏ Gala
❏ Telephone ❏ Lighting ❏ Cleanup ❏ Laundry

OR

_____
_____

Do you have access to a pickup or other truck which you might lend or drive for production errands? ❏ Yes ❏ No

Any medical or physical conditions that may affect your working any of the above? _____

For Director's Use Only

---

people afterward. Don't ask for too much; people may start leaving sections blank. If you do need a lot of information, give choices that can be checked quickly. (You'll see some good examples in the illustration.) No one form can serve the needs of every theater company. The one shown here is one solution. However, it omits items that others might want, such as age, height, and weight.

It also omits previous experience. That's because the Poorhouse Players uses a separate form for company membership, on which performing and technical experience is detailed. This membership form is permanent and is updated each time a member auditions, allowing the audition form to be used by the director and then discarded.

Section 3, the "Agreement," reads: "I understand that if I am cast in this production, I will not participate in any other theatrical production for six weeks prior to opening night. I understand that exceptions will be made only with the approval of the director." This is followed by a line for the actor's signature. The Players added this agreement to avoid the problem of performers overcommitting themselves and interfering with rehearsals.

Under "Skill Summary," the actor is quizzed about areas of production on which he or she will work. It also asks if the actor has access to a truck (always useful in community theater) and if there are any physical or medical conditions that may prevent the actor from working on any production tasks. This latter point is important. If someone has a bad back, you can't expect him or her to be lifting platforms into place. You always can assign them to work on some less physically strenuous task, such as publicity.

The space for director's comments is not large, but adequate for short notes about the auditioner to help the director in callbacks or casting. This form was produced using PageMaker, but any desktop publishing or forms software can be used. If you use a typewriter, lay out the form first, using a ruler and a fine-line felt-tip black pen. Then type in the wording. Use twelve-pitch type. If you create your form on a computer, keep the type size to 10-point or larger.

Good forms are an art form all their own. Before printing the final version, give a sample to several volunteers or staff members and ask them to fill it out. Ask also for comments. If they say there isn't enough space to write, or instructions are confusing, make adjustments accordingly. And if you find many auditioners don't understand some portion of the form, make changes before using the form again.

20 | *Putting Out the Welcome Mat*

Make Actors Comfortable When They Audition

David Spencer

*A*uditions are inherently uncomfortable for most actors, interfering with their desire to give you their best, and keeping you, the director, from an accurate assessment of their abilities. But a director can make an actor feel thoroughly appreciated and glad he did the audition (whether or not he gets the part), all without compromising an ounce of authority. If you create a climate in which the actor can thrive, the actor will benefit—and you'll get a better, more accurate reading. Here's how.

Even before audition day, I like to schedule five minutes more per audition than I think I'll need. When the actor sees the schedule, he or she will realize there is a little more room to breathe and lay in a foundation, rather than pinning everything on the hit-or-miss tricks of a quick kill. If this ultimately means an extra day of auditions, or longer audition days, so be it. The results are worth it.

In the waiting room, post—or better yet, photocopy and distribute—a page or two about the play. It should be a carefully written synopsis—as compared to the terse, standard breakdown—one that reveals as much as possible about the story, characters, and tone of the piece. If the actor has not been given the entire script beforehand, this simple handout helps focus concentration on what's needed, whether a character choice or the right audition song from a prepared repertoire. (If the handout can be picked up by the actors in advance, or distributed to them via fax or mail, so much the better.)

Make the actors' waiting area as comfortable and welcoming as possible. When the environment is uncontrollable, have your production assistant periodically step out and say, with a smile, something like, "We're sorry about the accommodations, folks." It helps enormously.

Greet the actors pleasantly. This is a two-step process. It begins when the production assistant goes to fetch each auditioner. The assistant is generally the mood-setting first contact an actor has with the production team, and should be cast as carefully as any role. You want someone friendly and outgoing as your assistant.

The second step involves the production team. Whether you shake hands individually or say that the assistant "shakes hands for all of us," do it with a light touch and a sense of humor. This is especially important if the actors are onstage and you're in the audience, which makes shaking hands nearly impossible.

Next: Break the ice. If the weather is brutal outside—hot, cold, or wet—thank the actor for braving it. If you remember an especially good performance or audition the actor gave previously, mention it. (If the weather is terrific and you've never seen the actor's work before, think of something else; you are, after all, on the "creative" team.) A warm greeting shows the actor your humanity; the icebreaker allows a small window for conversation, and most actors are smart enough not to abuse the privilege.

This does much more than ease some of the pressure on the actor. It gives you a little glimpse into the actor's personality. It's important to remember that the audition begins the moment the actor enters the room and doesn't end until the actor leaves. Actors are not just selling their talent; they're selling themselves. If you keep your mind open, what an actor shows you when not performing can be just as informative as the prepared material. It's not unheard of for an actor to land a role because of some revealing human moment: an aside, a joke, or a reaction to a mistake.

Which brings us to mistakes and mishaps. A voice cracks, a line is flubbed, a song choice isn't quite right, a piece of direction is misinterpreted. In most cases, mistakes shouldn't matter; it's how you and they deal with it that's important. The actor usually will be self-conscious enough to apologize for it. Wave it away convincingly or brush it off with a joke ("You'll have to do a lot worse than that to screw up!"). The actor will be relieved, further letting you take note of what missteps (if any) follow, providing a more three-dimensional picture of the actor's intelligence, responsiveness, and rehearsal demeanor. Only one kind of mistake should be taken seriously: the one that betrays a negative or disruptive attitude. Even then, there's rarely any point to regarding the actor frostily. It'll be over soon enough and the actor won't be called back.

When the actor is performing, don't take notes or whisper to your colleagues. If an actor is hitting one false chord after another, not even in the ballpark, cover your impatience. They're working hard for no pay and you owe their efforts the respect of a fair hearing.

There's no perfect phrase for turning down an actor's offer to try something again or to show you more. But there's one phrase—and its variants—to avoid at all costs: "That's not necessary. We know what you can do."

Actually, you don't. You don't know the actor's full range. You know what you saw and you extrapolated from that to the limits of your imagination. "We know what you can do" is a smug, insulting, arrogant statement. Imagine someone saying to you, "I saw half of that workshop scene. I know what you can direct." And think about your reaction.

It might be better to say, "That's not necessary. I think you've shown me what I need to know."

If you don't hold open auditions at which actors read scenes with each other, provide someone who reads expressively enough to give the actor something to work with and sensitively enough to respond in kind. There is a theory that bland, boilerplate, or unobtrusive readers are desirable, because they don't distract attention from the actor. But a theatrically charged reading provides one of the best ways to observe an actor's reflexes.

Sometimes an actor auditions brilliantly, but is simply wrong for the play; not because of a bad artistic decision, but because casting the role that way wouldn't make sense. This requires a judgment call, but occasionally you can say so, right on the spot. If pulled off with sensitivity, respect, and empathy, the actor will be grateful for the honesty.

Finally, let the actor feel it was worth the ride. Say goodbye as warmly as you said hello. If the actor has brought packages, a briefcase, or a purse, or if his or her music remains at the piano, have the assistant make note of that. Actors are sometimes forgetful in their nervousness; if they are reminded of their property or helped with it, they don't have to return later.

Stories of such courtesies spread throughout the acting community just as quickly as stories about abuse. If you have a reputation for holding pleasant auditions, it increases your available talent pool. It's gratifying to learn that a good actor said: "I didn't get the job, but they sure hold great auditions!"

Eight Things to
Look for in
Auditions

21

Questions to Ask
About the Actors
Who Want a Role

W hen casting a show, ask yourself the following
questions about each actor who auditions.

1. *Does the actor fit the theatrical requirements
of the role?* This usually is the easiest question to deal with; after all, a male role normally calls for a male actor, a female
role for a female actor. But sometimes a director is hampered
by traditional casting. It's better to look beyond the tried-and-
true, if only to increase your options.

2. *Is there some spark in the actor's personality that suggests
the character?* It's true that you seldom find an actor who reads
or looks 100 percent of what you want by performance date,
but the right actor for the part should show an understanding
of the character in question. For example, watch how the
actor walks to and from the audition stage, and how he or she
interacts with others in the room, including yourself.

3. *Does the actor's voice and speech pattern suggest the part?*
When in doubt, explain how you might want the character to
speak, and see if the actor can come close to that. Or suggest
the actor try different vocal patterns of his or her own
devising.

4. *Does the actor have the physical appearance for the part?*
Or, if not, could he or she suggest it, given makeup and
costume? Again, if possible, tell the actor something about
the way you visualize the character, and ask him or her to try
ways to suggest those attributes.

5. *How does the audition audience (assuming you have one) react to the actor in question?* If the scene is comic, does the actor draw laughs? If dramatic, does the actor keep the audience's attention? While some directors prefer private auditions, there is much to be said for open tryouts in order to gauge an actor's impact on those watching.

6. *What can be made of the actor's stage presence and poise?* Self-assurance is essential if an actor is to be believable in a part, even if the character being played has no self-assurance at all.

7. *Does the actor have flexibility and an ability to take direction?* When comparing actors, give strong, clear directions for a particular scene and see how they follow through. Remember, if an actor can't take direction well at this point, he or she won't do well in rehearsal, either. All other qualifications being equal, the ability to take direction is reason enough to cast one actor over another.

8. *Are there any conflicts in the actor's schedule that might create problems with rehearsals?* Many directors have cast the "ideal" actor only to find that frequent tardiness or absences crippled the show or lowered cast morale.

Audition the Actor, Not the Part

22

Use Auditions to Bring Out the Best in Auditioners, Experienced or Not

"Wh9at you want from an audition is to maximize the amount of information you can glean about and from an actor in the shortest period of time." We suspect that most directors would agree with director Ted Strickland in this. However, we also know that, for many, auditions are at best a chore and at worst an abiding frustration. That's why we were struck by the very different approach Strickland has used at Tennessee's Chattanooga Little Theatre, particularly when we watched it in action.

No More Readings

"The usual way of doing things is for people to walk in, fill out forms, and read from the script," Strickland points out. "You find out how well they *read*, not how well they act. The problem is that some people just can't read. They learn and speak lines beautifully, but you don't find this out at auditions and so you lose them right off."

Others audition well but never develop in the part, he adds. Still others are new to the stage and their awkwardness often masks latent talent.

"Auditions should help the director determine an actor's

potential—movement, voice, range, and projection. You want to know if they can take direction, relate to other people, and if they can create a character."

To identify these critical skills, Strickland puts a new twist on the familiar process of general auditions and callbacks. Those who attend general auditions are not asked to read from a script or prepare a monologue. Instead, they find themselves doing a series of informal exercises and improvs in an environment that minimizes distractions. Those who make the cut are asked to callbacks, where for the first time they work with the script.

Not only does this system work for the director, but the actors like it, too. In addition, Strickland says it has rejuvenated the company by opening it up to more new talent—and new audiences.

Environment

Strickland focuses first on improving the audition environment.

"Most audition spaces are intimidating," he points out. "People are tense. And anything that signals negatively can affect them." That's why it is important for there to be a greeter at the door to pay attention to newcomers, he says. At the same time, the director or other staff should make an effort not to single out oldtimers, either.

"Greet everyone with equal enthusiasm," he says. "Otherwise, you give the impression that yours is a closed group, where new people aren't welcome. Try to create an environment that is welcoming. Remember, you need to get rid of tension before an actor can produce."

Keep the audition space as open and as uncluttered as possible. Minimize clutter and other distractions. Make sure you can see those waiting, as well those who are actually auditioning; you can learn a lot about people when they're not "on."

For Starters

Strickland starts the audition by relaxing the actors with some freeform exercises that also help him evaluate people without their knowing it. He prefers to work with groups of six to ten auditioners at a time. They feel safer and thus more relaxed. It's also a more efficient use of time.

We watch as he invites a group of actors to come up and stand with their back to one wall. He asks each person to walk across the room, then skip back. ("It's a chance to have everyone look ridiculous—and everyone is in the same boat," he tells us later.) There's a lot of nervous laughter and the ice is broken. At the same time, this simple exercise indicates both coordination and inhibition.

Then Strickland tells each person to walk in a particular way:

"Someone has been spreading vicious stories about you. They are on the other side of the room from you—walk over to them."

"You've just been fired from your job and you are walking into your home to confront the person you live with."

"You just received the best news you've ever received and are going to tell a friend."

"You are God's gift to the opposite sex; walk in a way that shows that."

This type of activity shows the interpretive process at work. "You'll see whether a person is willing to try something," he says. "A person doesn't have to be a trained actor to do this kind of thing well, so it gives you a feeling for his or her potential. And as for experienced actors, you'll find those who show you a character rather than *be* a character. Try physical things. Have them walk or whatever in a way consistent with a particular character. If you want, ask them to do several different walks. The differences each time show whether they can act or take direction."

Group Effort

Another reason for auditioning people in groups is that "You can do ten people in four minutes," Strickland points out. "It also keeps people from sitting too long. When you do readings at auditions, people sit and get fidgety. So a group audition is more efficient and makes people feel more comfortable."

Strickland sometimes uses the familiar "red light, green light" game, but with the players as characters.

"Again, it reduces tension. It's something they probably know, and they actually have fun. Participants develop a relationship through competition. You can see how fast people learn."

We saw what Strickland means as we watch some auditioners play the game. The first time he calls out two "red lights" in a row, the players seem confused. They apparently assumed that a "red light" would be followed by a "green light." They soon begin to concentrate, to listen more carefully.

"Such an exercise identifies those actors who second–guess what the director wants," he says, laughing. "Seriously, though, control is important to an actor, and so is the ability to learn. This exercise focuses on those traits."

Later, he has five people mime a game of dodge ball in slow motion. The game shows each person's ability to react, to play off the others. Because no ball actually exists, each person has to focus on who has it at any given moment to keep things moving smoothly. The exercise also shows whether a person can function as part of an ensemble.

Readings with a Difference

So far, not a word has been spoken by any of those auditioning. Not all activity is physical, however. Strickland next gives eight people a newspaper page each. He asks them to select any paragraph and read it aloud. Then he asks them to read the randomly chosen paragraph in various ways—consoling a small child, picking up someone in a bar, firing someone, scolding a child, proposing marriage, telling a ghost story.

"This really shows versatility, voice quality, the ability to take direction, basic technique," he explains. "And no one has the advantage of preparation. A newspaper also avoids the problem of actors hearing the same scene over and over, which affects their own interpretation. Each time is different. You also may find speech patterns that are unusual and could be used in some way to add variety to your production."

Strickland advises that you also observe those who are *not* reading as well. Actors who don't focus, who shut down when they're not speaking, or who engage in conversation could cause problems if cast.

Improvs with a Twist

Strickland also uses improvisational techniques. In one improv, a wife suspects her husband of having an affair. They confront each other—but speak only in numbers.

He: 7
She: 7?
He: 7
She: (Shaking head.) 8, 12, 14
He: *14?*
She: 14!

"Improv is a great technique," Strickland says, "but actors often try to become playwrights. That's why I have them speak in numbers or letters. It takes the script away from them and forces them to play the situation. You'll see what kind of resources they can draw on and something about their thought processes. Don't let the improv go on too long: stop them when they get in a rut or don't take the scene to a new level."

Improvs are "a great equalizer," he adds. "They get around the problem you sometimes encounter where some people are doing a cold reading, while others are already familiar with the script.

"Auditions should be fair—or at least be perceived as fair," Strickland says. "That's why I like using these exercises. They treat everyone equally. Just as important, they help you separate the wheat from the chaff. In community theater, you often get people with no or little ability. If you have them *all* read, you'll be there all night."

Groundwork, Ground Rules, and Unexpected Benefits

Strickland spends a day making lists of activities to use in auditions. He doesn't set a particular order of use, but makes that call as he observes the people who have shown up. It's important to have a number of activities on which to draw, he says, because "the effect is cumulative. That is, the auditioners show themselves through several exercises. You need to observe them carefully as they go through the activities."

Strickland uses the same methods to audition children and adults. "Children respond well to the use of games and exercises," he says. "It's especially helpful because they often don't have a lot of theater experience. So having them walk like an animal, for instance, appeals to them.

"A lot of adult actors, especially those who are great readers, don't like doing these games and exercises. Some even resent it, but know they have to go through it to get to callbacks. But I learn something about people every time, including actors I've used before. It's really great to get people to do something different."

One inviolable rule for both children and adults: Only those actually auditioning may be present.

"Auditions are closed because onlookers can be distracting. Especially parents. Even if they don't say anything, their presence distracts. And I want the person auditioning to be focused."

For musicals, Strickland has half the group sing while the other half learns a dance combination. "Reading may be less important in a musical," he says. "If they can't *sing* the part, they can't play the part."

Callbacks

Exercises at general auditions solve the problem of having enough scripts handy or selecting audition scenes. Then, at callbacks, when you have a smaller group, you can work with them using the script and actual characterizations. The purpose of the audition exercises is to ensure that callbacks are productive and don't waste time, Strickland says.

"For callbacks, plan so you know precisely what people will read. Take the choice element out. I do not ask people if they want to read for a particular part at callbacks. I tell them, 'You may or may not read the part you want. That's OK. I don't cast that way.' " And I mean it. By this point, I know what I want, and I have a pretty good idea of what most of the actors can do. It's down to specifics. I don't have to have each person read a specific role to find out what they're capable of. I *may* have someone read a part to see if they can give me the voice quality I'm looking for, perhaps, but there's no point in reading more than is needed to give the director what he or she wants to know."

Final Thoughts

One of the less obvious benefits of Strickland's audition methods is that it generates new performers for his company.

"At least one–third of any cast of mine is always brand new. That's because I'm not relying on cold readings any more; I can spot potential without that."

As a result, the perception of the community is that Chattanooga Little Theatre is an open group, an evolving group. Just as important, Strickland points out, new people in the cast means new people in the audience—and at the next audition.

"If you don't get new folks in, you might as well declare yourself a nonpaid repertory company."

It's a win-win situation. The company benefits, the director finds casting to be more relaxed and productive, and those who audition enjoy themselves as well.

"People come up and say, 'Even if I don't get a part, I had fun,' " Strickland says.

When was the last time you heard that about *your* company's auditions?

The Seven Warning Signs of Auditions

Look Out for Actors with These Behaviors

Y ou've prepared well, gotten the word out, and gotten a good turnout. You've run your audition well and gotten a good sense of the skill level of your potential actors. You've begun to formulate in your mind whether certain actors will be right for particular roles. But talent, skill, and appropriateness are only some of what you should be looking for at the audition.

Look Out for Actors with These Behaviors

Every moment counts at an audition. A director has only a short time to evaluate each actor's suitability for the roles being cast. Aside from the question of talent, your judgments often are made under stress and with little opportunity to determine who will be easy to work with during the rehearsal period. We asked directors to share their advice, which we pass on in the form of some audition warning signs that may help flag potential difficulties.

Like the warning signs of a serious illness, however, remember that these indicate the *possibility* of a problem. To help you remember them, we have broken them down into memorable character types. If you spot any one of them, you may want to do some follow-up—with the actor or with someone who may have worked with him or her—before making any casting decision.

1. The Expert ■ This first type is the one who knows the play inside and out, and will make that quite clear to you—sometimes telling you so on the audition form or to your face. You also can spot this type because he nods or shakes his head while you explain the play or while other actors are auditioning, as if to say, "that's the right way" or "that's the wrong way." Often these actors will give good auditions because they are so familiar with the play. The problem is that they may have a rigid idea of how the show should be directed, one that may clash with your own vision. If you do cast such a person, be up front with him or her. Explain that you will be directing the play *your* way and, while you welcome input from your actors, you expect to have the last word. As you do this, watch facial expression and body language; if you sense resistance, reconsider your choice.

2. The Disturbing Influence ■ While most actors have a need to be noticed, there are some whose need borders on the disturbed. During auditions, watch and listen carefully for any behavior that seems out of sync. Nervousness, for example, is common at auditions, but strange behavior is another matter. At one audition we attended, we saw a young woman whose reactions and facial expressions were overexaggerated. When she asked questions of the director, it was not simply to get information—she clearly wanted attention. She gave a good reading, but her energy level was almost manic. This alone might not strike her from consideration, but a few phone calls to those who had worked with her confirmed that these were indeed signs of some emotional instability.

At a different audition, one of the actors complained of a fly buzzing—not once, but to every person who came into the room. She then proceeded to hunt loudly for something to kill the fly. She might as well have worn a flashing neon sign saying, "NOTICE ME." The director, wisely, did not cast her.

3. The Unprepared ■ If actors have been asked to prepare a scene or a song, but give every indication that they have not taken time to do so, you need to ask yourself, "Is this person serious about a commitment to this show?" Some actors feel if they know the director, they don't need to work hard at audition because "He knows what I can do." But after one actor stumbled miserably through an audition song, a director confided to her assistant, "I felt insulted that he didn't think this was important enough to come better prepared." Under such a circumstance, don't waste your time feeling insulted. Rather, consider whether such behavior may indicate an attitude problem that will come back to haunt you during rehearsals.

4. The Isolationist ■ Beware the actor who ignores what is going on during the auditions. Such a person may be buried in the script, reading a novel, or talking to someone else. A good actor watches what others in the audition are doing and listens attentively to what the director says. This attention to detail not only helps an actor do a better job in the reading, but also is the keystone to a good working relationship with you during rehearsals. The person who isolates himself from others during auditions also may have problems becoming part of the performance team. The talker ignores the proceedings just as much as the reader, and the same concerns apply. But the reader only prevents one person from doing a good job; the talker prevents somebody else as well. Consider whether you want to deal with either variety of Isolationist in the weeks to come.

5. The Dimsighted ■ Often directors will ask if anyone wishes to read a part for which they have not already auditioned. This is usually done out of courtesy, although it does sometimes flush out the actor with heretofore hidden talent. It's our experience this also can flush out the problem people, or at least confirm your suspicions. That's because problem people often ask to read something for which they are clearly not suited, which could indicate that they (a) have unrealistic expectations, (b) are totally self-absorbed, (c) think they are more talented than they really are, or (d) all of the above. Such people can cause discipline problems when you begin to help them create their characterization.

6. The Repeat Offender ■ If you ask actors to read a part in a certain way, or try a different characterization, pay close attention. First, look for any sign that they are *trying* to do what you ask. Many actors freeze in this mode because they know that the director is now looking for something *specific* instead of a generalized reading. If possible, give the actor a chance to go off and try some things in private, then return and try again. However, if you get the same reading a second time, there's a good chance that you have a one-note performer or an actor who does not take direction well—a liability in either case.

7. The "Perfect" Reading ■ The seventh situation is somewhat related to the previous one. Sometimes someone gives an exceptional reading for a particular role and also seems to have the look and presence of the character. Although all seems perfect, protect yourself by asking the actor to read a part for which he or she is *not* being considered, even if it seems ludicrous to do so. What you want to look for is *any* indication that they can give a different reading and produce a different character from that which attracted you in the first place. The reason is simple: You want more from an actor than what they gave in audition. In this way, this case is similar to the Repeat Offender. Again, you will be working with the person to develop and deepen the characterization; to do that, the actor will need flexibility.

We saw such a situation when the director asked two males to read a female part in the play. The difference was astonishing. One actor was embarrassed, his performance tentative and wooden. The other dropped whatever inhibitions he may have had and *became* the woman in question. The choice was clear.

While these warning signs are just that, signs, as a director, the same powers of observation you use to guide a play in progress also can help assure that you get off to the right start.

Children Will Listen | 24

Auditioning children is significantly different than auditioning adults. It means dealing with parents as well, it means adjusting your expectations, and, most important, it means being aware of the emotional, physical, and stylistic qualities children will bring to an audition. One of the most important ways a director can help prepare children for an audition is to convey to parents how they can help and what is expected of them. Here is some advice from the newsletter of The Little Theater of Winston-Salem in North Carolina.

How to Prepare Young People for Auditions

LEE MORGAN

*H*aving a child in a play is a commitment on the part not only of the child, but also of the parents. Performing in a play can be a tremendously rewarding and educational experience for a child. He or she can learn valuable lessons about responsibility and teamwork, and about the rewards of a job well done. These lessons can be well worth the cost in terms of time and effort.

However, there are special problems involved when children audition for plays. Auditions, of course, are a tense situation for everyone, and children often have not developed the maturity and poise necessary to handle the pressure of auditions gracefully.

But there are things that parents can do to make the situation a little easier for their children. You might make these known to them as part of an audition information packet. It will make life easier for everyone. Here's what we at The Little Theatre told parents before an audition for *Annie*:

■ *Be sure your child knows what to expect.* Find out what is likely to happen during the audition and discuss it with the child. Find out about the process and explain it step by step.

At The Little Theatre, we audition children for musicals as a group. All auditioners are taken into the audition room, where they are taught part of one of the songs from the score. They sing the song through as a group until everyone knows it well, then they go around the circle, with each child singing by himself or herself. Then they go through the same routine with a dance combination.

We do this to put the children at ease and give them a way to present themselves at their best with a minimum of stress and anxiety. This also gives us the opportunity to see how the child responds in a learning situation that is not unlike rehearsals.

■ *Your child should be prepared to audition without you in the room.* This is often very hard for parents, particularly when they have been involved closely in the audition preparations. However, we have found that children are less inhibited and react more spontaneously and freely when parents are not present. And because non-cast members do not attend rehearsals, having the parents not present during the audition gives a director a better idea of how the child will respond in rehearsals.

■ *Do not make the audition more important than it really is.* For *Annie* auditions, we expect to see eighty to one hundred girls for the seven available roles. Everyone who auditions cannot be cast— which is a fact of theatrical life for actors of all ages. Your child should know that not being chosen is not a failure. Explain that very often casting choices are made on the basis of considerations other than talent. Your child should understand that if a director has multiple choices for a particular part, she might decide on one person because they look "right" for the role, or because they are the "right" height to go with other cast members, or because she had to decide on one person and flipped a coin. You should explain to your child that not being cast is not the end of the world, nor should it make her feel bad about herself.

Double, Double . . .

25

Not only do you need to deal somewhat differently with children during the audition process, you also may want to consider an entirely different casting procedure with them. While double-casting can and has been used in adult theater, it is particularly well adapted to youth theater.

It May Create Toil and Trouble, But Often Double-Casting Makes Sense

DIANE CREWS

M any directors are noticeably fearful of double-casting a show. From my perspective, however, there is really no reason for such fear. In the past four years, I have partially or fully double-cast all twelve of the shows I've directed, and have lived to write about it.

Why would anyone even consider such a practice? There are many reasons, but what really got me started was my desire not to appear onstage with little or no notice. When an actor became ill during a production at York [Pennsylvania] Little Theatre of *Babes in Toyland*, I had to take over the part of the singing ingenue, which had been played by a very tall, svelte, male actor. I'm none of the above, and had two hours to prepare and get a costume together. I did the entire performance, deleting only the bit where he changed his shirt onstage. By the curtain call, I had aged considerably.

The very next show, the horse in James Still's *Velveteen*

Rabbit got strep throat just prior to opening. This time, the part was played by a young woman and the costume did fit, but that was it for me. I began trying to find viable ways to avoid stepping into parts on a regular basis.

Being involved, as I am, in youth theater probably makes double-casting easier. While other directors seem to have enough auditioners to cast well only once, I have plenty of actors from which to choose. For a musical version of *The Little Princess*, I had no trouble getting two equal casts of twenty-six from the 215 hopefuls I saw. Before a dear friend kicked me, I was even considering trying three casts.

When there is so much interest (I usually have about 150 on average at auditions), it's very hard not to include as many actors as possible—while still producing the best show you can. Double-casting can succeed with any group, but works especially well with community and youth theater. If your run is short, it may not prove to be practical, but with a larger number of performances, the down time per cast serves the production well.

The Positives

There are many other benefits to double-casting:

- *It allows for a greater number of actors to participate and learn.*

- *It provides the production with built-in understudies.* The show can always go on.

- *It makes it possible for cast members to participate in other activities.* John can be in the show and attend his business seminar on Saturday afternoon because Jake is doing the matinee anyway. Amy doesn't have to choose between the show and her choir because she can switch with Suzanne and not miss her concert.

- *It heightens the potential for ensemble work.* Working with at least twice as many as would be the norm, you have a greater need to incorporate group activities that create and enhance the team spirit necessary for a production. The equalizing effect of being one of many also adds to the group dynamic.

- *It increases the cast's flexibility.* When you have frequent exposure to the work of different actors, you become a less restricted actor yourself. When Joe has a flat tire and Amos fills in opposite Janice, who is used to Joe, she learns to respond to a different character interpretation.

■ *It enhances the entire company's concentration.* Ruth always enters when John runs his left hand through his hair. Andy doesn't use that particular gesture. Ruth and the entire cast must listen and observe carefully so they can concentrate and not break character.

■ *It allows the second actor you would have called for the part to have an opportunity to play it.*

The Negatives

Before you jump into it, however, let me add that there can be difficulties with double-casting. First, it decreases the rehearsal time per actor and increases the work and stress for the director. It also requires more creativity from the costume designer and careful and complicated scheduling. And it's possible you'll give the perception that one cast or actor is weaker than the other. Plays that need a great deal of timing (for instance, farces) and dramas that depend on detailed script analysis, or any show that demands special dramatic skills, also may suffer from double-casting,

Some of these problems can be minimized by different kinds of double-casting—because there are several types. Complete double-casting means casting two entirely separate groups of actors. But there's also partial, where you double-cast your major parts and single-cast the others, if the quality of your actors is uneven and you have some particularly prominent characters. You can also double from within. The entire cast will be in the show every night, but will play different parts every other performance. For example, I doubled the eight shortest of the thirteen dwarves in *The Hobbit*, who played the elves in alternating performances.

What I call *conglomerate doubling* is when you mix and match any and all of the above. For example, Martha Cratchit in *A Christmas Carol* was doubled by Sarah and Julie. Sometimes they simply switched between Martha and a townswoman. However, when Julie, who was also a student musical conductor, was in the pit, then Sarah played the part of Martha, Liz was the townswoman, and Jane danced with Bill at Fezziwigs!

As you can see, this can become very complicated. My schedule sometimes seems like a space launch. And, as I've indicated, double-casting doesn't prevent all problems. One winter, on opening night of a musical *Robin Hood*, there was a blizzard. As the calls came in, I was doing all right until both women who played Mother Megs called. Although I had doubled every part, I still ended up with two actors playing the same role who couldn't make it to the theater.

Now, in addition to size and talent, I consider geography when casting in the winter.

In the beginning, this new process seemed strange and required some philosophical adjustments. If you double-cast, you always must remember that one cast is not understudying the other. Both casts are equal and must be treated accordingly. Don't forget, also, that the lines, blocking, music, and choreography are the same per character and that each actor is responsible for developing his or her own character.

Step by Step

If you do go ahead and try double-casting, keep your auditioning procedures the same as always. You simply need to add an awareness of your intent to double-cast. At most auditions, there are at least two actors who could do each part. I used to hold on to both audition forms until I was sure one had said yes. Now, I simply cast them both.

Casting is also similar to normal procedures. You just need to do it twice. It gets easier with each show—honest. The larger parts and those needing specific talents will need to be cast according to ability, but the others can be organized with the costumer's needs in mind. Secondary characters and chorus members can be doubled by height and size, thus allowing for shared costumes.

Rehearsing is the area requiring the greatest amount of creativity and patience from the director and cooperation from the cast. Your rehearsal space does not get larger just because you decide to double-cast. Knowing that you're going to be squished together for three or four weeks until you get onstage is a reality to be dealt with and accepted before you schedule rehearsals.

Check space availability and then try to organize full cast rehearsals when no one else needs the building, so stage managers can rehearse scenes or take the other cast to alternate spaces. When the weather is nice, don't hesitate to work outside once everyone is familiar with the ground plan. If you're not double-casting from within, break the show up even more carefully than you usually do. You do not want hordes of actors sitting idle.

Blocking is a challenge and can take many forms. You can get Cast A up and give them the blocking while Cast B watches and writes it down. Then Cast B runs through that scene while Cast A watches. The process then begins again with Cast B up first. Try to alternate Cast A and Cast B as often as possible.

Another approach is shadowing. When space allows, get both casts up at once, and let them walk the blocking together, but with each having a chance to be in front and say the lines. If you find that those on the sidelines do not use their downtime productively, and you are saying everything twice anyway, then bring them in and work separately. It's double time for you, but it could save your sanity.

Allow for the casts to mix as needed. The flexibility of having two of everything can save many a rehearsal and performance.

Scheduling performances for each cast can be done a number of ways. I try to make it as simple and consistent as possible. Start to schedule each cast for every other performance, and then make the necessary adjustments to assure that each has a Friday night, a matinee, and so on.

The most critical part of scheduling is to make the information available as soon as possible, and do your very best not to change it. I include it on the rehearsal schedule that is distributed at the read-through.

One final pointer: Make sure your box office has a copy of who's performing at which performance. People will be calling who want to see a particular cast. We have some audience members who get tickets for both so they can enjoy the differences. That's because you will end up with two different productions of the same play. Neither is better than the other, but they will be different.

Working with large, multigenerational casts, doubling has become a way of life for me. Now, when I have an occasional single actor per part, *that* requires an adjustment.

26 | *Everyone Onstage*

As the effects of the Americans with Disabilities Act (ADA) has filtered down to every level and aspect of our society over the last decade, more and more theaters have tried to become inclusive in their auditioning and casting policies. (Not to mention how it has affected their physical plant and their adaptations to audience members and others.) And some have been wondering how they can become more inclusive—and whether, in fact, it's worth it.

Why Casting Actors with Disabilities Is in Everyone's Best Interest

NANCIANNE PFISTER

*I*n small but increasing numbers, disabled and able-bodied actors are sharing the stage in theaters across the country. There are many reasons for this development, but also the common denominator seems to be the realization that excluding disabled actors (intentionally or not) is not only unfair, but also foolish. After all, most directors are delighted to have an abundance of talented performers at auditions. Why would they limit the pool of available talent by not including performers with disabilities in their search for the best cast?

Why settle for an able-bodied mezzo-soprano who will be adequate if you can cast one who will sing "You'll Never Walk Alone" brilliantly from her wheelchair? Can the bitter Willy Loman be hearing-impaired? Must all 12 angry men be sighted? Is Regina Giddens less evil on crutches?

The answer to all of these, of course, is "no," which is why

110

you'll find able-bodied and disabled actors sharing the stage at many theaters across the country.

Dropping Barriers

"We believe that everyone is entitled to all of life's activities, including the performing arts, and we are taking a leading role in making that happen," says Walter Born, founding director of Creative Productions in Aberdeen, New Jersey.

In 1988, as a special project, Born created Theatre of Celebration. Seeking to integrate disabled actors with able-bodied players, the concept has been so successful that it is no longer a separate project, just another show in the season.

One of the first barriers Theatre of Celebration faced was literary, not physical. In New York, where he had been a working actor, Born was told repeatedly to "Get lost!" when he requested freedom to make script changes in order to accommodate nontraditional actors.

Fortunately, he found help through Very Special Arts, a national association for disabled performers headquartered at The Kennedy Center in Washington, DC. Each year, VSA sponsors the Henry Fonda Young Playwright's Project, in which students aged twelve to eighteen write scripts about disability. The two scripts judged the best are produced at The Kennedy Center. Born received permission to use these winning scripts that otherwise might be "just filed away and forgotten." He now had a resource for original appropriate material.

Rod Lathim of Access Theatre in Santa Barbara, California, which closed its doors in 1996, also made use of original material— by allowing his performers to write their own scripts. Recently, the play *Storm Reading* was not only produced by Access Theatre, but also taken on tour and videotaped for a PBS special. The script is by Neil Marcus, a disabled playwright who also appears in the production. Another original script from Access Theatre, *Flight*, premiered at the national conference of the Association for Theatre & Accessibility one year in Atlanta.

In Denver, the Physically Handicapped Amateur Musical Actors League (PHAMALy) integrates performers who have disabilities ranging from impaired hearing to cerebral palsy. It is an extra challenge for any choreographer to stage a production number in which some of the dancers are in wheelchairs. However, one of the missions of PHAMALy is to train theater professionals to expand their creative capabilities, finding ways to adapt to nontraditional performers.

In New York City, Theatre by the Blind has presented original works since 1984. Productions have involved blind, partially sighted, and sighted performers. Likewise, Cleveland's Signstage Theatre and Chicago's Centerlight Theatre routinely cast their productions with actors who have varying degrees of hearing loss.

Casting Concerns

One issue of concern is the way scripts are chosen and cast. Actors with disabilities often are shut out of consideration for two quite opposing reasons. Often, if the playwright has written a disability into the script, the director will choose an able-bodied actor for the role—an actor who must then work to simulate the condition. On the other hand, few directors think of casting a talented actor with a disability in a role that is not expressly written as such.

This does not mean, however, that a director must search for plays featuring characters who are disabled, says Lathim. "Disabled people live in the same world as the rest of us and do all the different things we do." In other words, most plays can be cast to include one actor with a disability, as we pointed out at the beginning of the article.

Indeed, Lathim, who was also president of the Association for Theatre & Accessibility, thinks the casting of nontraditional performers should no longer be an issue. He offers advice to companies that will have a disabled performer onstage for the first time.

"Know that there are all kinds of people in the world," he says. "If you create work that is inclusive, issues of disability go out the window. The director should look upon casting a disabled actor as an opportunity to add dimension to a role. And no explanation is required. The character is under no obligation to explain the disability by saying a truck hit him twelve years ago anymore than he has to explain his blue eyes. It's just part of who he is."

Particular attention must be paid to school productions, according to Lathim. If a disabled student auditions, the director/teacher must abide by the ADA and give that student every opportunity to succeed. Increasingly, teachers will encounter talented students who need physical accommodation if they are to perform with able-bodied students. It's the director's job to make that accommodation a creative challenge, not an accessibility hassle.

Lathim also rejects the stereotype of the long-suffering disabled saint, whose monumental patience is an inspiration to all. "I know deaf people who are jerks, just as I know hearing people who are jerks. And why not let a disabled person play the villain? Why do some directors find that difficult?"

Lathim emphasizes that keeping the lines of communication open will get the best performance from a disabled artist, as it does with any actor. Set this pattern from the beginning by creating audition notices that let performers with disabilities know they will be welcome.

Creative Options

Directors should avoid making a "can't do" list for any disabled performer until they talk with the actor. It's better to operate on the principle that disabled actors can do anything anyone else can until they tell you otherwise. Accommodations are most successful when they are determined jointly by director and actor.

One common need, no matter what the disability, is for extended rehearsal time. Born allows an extra twenty-five percent for Theatre of Celebration rehearsals, but insists that actors be disciplined enough to do much of their work away from the rehearsal space.

Deaf or hearing-diminished actors who do not read lips or wear a hearing aid will need extra time for directions to be signed. Directors who are not signers should remember to speak to the actor, not the interpreter.

Actors with acute vision problems can become familiar with the surroundings more quickly if they are first guided around the empty stage, as well as into the green room and other backstage areas. Later, as other actors come onstage, it is easier to adjust. (If the actor has a guide dog, do not touch or speak to it. A working guide dog is not a pet.)

Often, time can be saved by using a buddy system, pairing the actor who has a disability with one who has none. This is especially true when children are involved.

Actors in wheelchairs need costumes without excess fabric that could become tangled in a wheel. This represents more danger to the costume than to the actor, but a jammed wheel will make it difficult for the actor to move across the stage.

"Costumers learn to use a lot of Velcro," says Lathim, citing one solution to difficulties in making quick changes for a performer who cannot stand unaided. Costumes must be constructed in such a way that they do not interfere with crutches, walkers, or canes.

When questions of convenience or safety arise, the disabled actor needs to be respected as the expert, according to Lathim. "Don't assume anything," he says. "These people are pros at adapting, so ask them what should be done."

Increasingly, they are being asked, as theater companies across the country encourage participation of all the talented artists available to them, no matter what the packaging.

27 | *The Moment of Truth*

Narrowing Down the Choices and Informing the Actors

No matter how well you've prepared, now matter how well organized you are, and no matter how efficiently you've run the audition itself, if your final decisions on whom you are casting for your production aren't made carefully, all the hard work may have been for naught. You must put in as much careful effort into those final decisions as you have into all that has gone before. After auditions, here's how to narrow down the choices and inform the actors.

Choosing a cast from many candidates can be both difficult and painful, but there are ways to make the task easier on you and on those whom you have auditioned. First, using notes you've taken during auditions and callbacks, eliminate the people you know you don't want or can't use. Then work through the cast list, starting with the lead roles, and note possibilities among the remaining candidates.

Many theater groups use an audition panel, particularly in the case of musicals. This not only gives the director additional points of view, but also gives those auditioning the impression (correct, we hope) that casting decisions won't be made arbitrarily. Such panels can be a big help to the director because they offer an opportunity to voice your thoughts about each candidate with your colleagues.

Casting is an inexact art and there are no simple answers to improving the selection process. Directors we talked with were quick to share some thoughts on the subject, however.

"Watch out for being bowled over by someone who gives

a complete performance," warns one experienced director. "What you see may be all you'll get. Often these actors never change or improve during rehearsal. They often don't take direction well, either. It's better to look for someone with potential, someone you can help work toward the characterization you want."

Keep an open mind, advises another director. "A hunch about an actor can be right, and an imperfect but exciting candidate may give, by opening night, a more compelling performance than a merely competent auditioner. Be ready to take some chances while avoiding blatant risks."

Rejections

There are many ways of letting people know they have not been cast. Letters are often the best method, because the message can be crafted carefully. Keep them short and do not give reasons for the rejection. Being turned down is painful and if you give reasons, an actor may want to argue the point with you. This doesn't get them—or you—anywhere. Be polite but firm. Do not antagonize anyone. You may want them to audition for future productions for which they may be more suitable.

Some theater companies phone all those who have auditioned. If you choose to do this, have it handled by someone other than the director. The auditioners may want to know why they were not cast and may try to dispute the decision. If the person calling can say honestly, "I don't know" or "I was not part of the casting decision," it makes matters easier for everyone involved.

Some companies make no other effort to notify auditioners than to post the cast list in a public place. While this system relieves the director or anyone else in the company of the bother of sending letters or making calls, it comes across as a cold, mechanical procedure. It is hard enough to deal with rejection without it being a public one. (We've known actors to avoid the notice area until they were sure no one else was around.) Another method, which is equally cold, is to list the cast on a voice-mail message. Instead, use the audition process to build goodwill for your company. Ideally, every actor who has auditioned should be told the outcome personally and privately, by letter or phone call. (Clearly, this is impractical in large-scale auditions. A mail-merge form letter is a reasonable alternative.)

Whichever method you choose to inform your people, ask those you have cast to inform you promptly of their acceptance (or otherwise) and give them the date, time, and place of the first rehearsal.

Write or phone successful candidates first; you may have to go back to your backup list if someone turns down a part.

If you have no one on the backup list to cast in a role, then it's time to call those people who did not audition but who might be able to handle the part. This is a sensitive process because if you do cast someone who didn't audition, those rejected may assume you had already precast some roles. To avoid this possibility, explain your company's casting policy (see Chapter 29) in the audition materials you hand out.

The Rejection Letter

The following rejection letter from Keith Martin, when he was artistic director of Theatre Charlotte in North Carolina, is a good example of a carefully crafted, sensitive, but to-the-point rejection notice.

> Dear Auditionee:
> On behalf of Theatre Charlotte, I want to thank you for giving so much of yourself in talent, time, energy, and excitement during recent auditions for *Dreamgirls*. Unfortunately, the limited number of roles made it impossible to cast everyone who auditioned; I regret not being able to utilize your particular talents in this production.
> Please do not let this discourage you. There are many roles available in the upcoming season, and Theatre Charlotte strongly advises you to audition again. Our next production is the Tony-Award–winning musical, *Follies*. Mark your calendar now for the pre-audition workshops on July 10 and 11, with auditions on July 17 and 18.
> Remember, theater is much more than what happens onstage. *Dreamgirls* is an enormous technical production and there are many creative tasks that must be completed before the actors can perform. So, for this production at least, please join us backstage. We would love to see you! A technical production schedule is enclosed for your information.
> As always, if you would like to discuss your audition, please do not hesitate to call for an appointment. Thank you again for your interest in Theatre Charlotte.

(The previous was a form letter. At the bottom, Martin wrote personal notes, as appropriate. One read, "Janet—I'm very pleased with your progress since your last audition, especially your monologue and preparation. Keep up the good work! —Keith")

Reforesting the Theater | 28

In addition to its sensitivity with its rejection letters, Theatre Charlotte some years ago employed a method that eased the pain of rejection—and let the theater take advantage of the talents of those it chose not to cast.

How to Develop Better Actors for Future Auditions

NANCIANNE PFISTER

*I*magine a low-cost theater program that boosts morale, builds acting skills, auditions guest directors, and brings older actors back to the stage. Fantasy? Not at all, although The Reading Stage program that was used by North Carolina's Theatre Charlotte some years ago had its genesis in a situation that many directors might term a "wonderful problem."

The problem: So many performers came to auditions that directors could cast a show several different ways. Unfortunately, they were allowed only one cast. What would happen to those who were not cast? How could the company keep their interest so they would return for the next auditions with greater hope of gaining a role?

"We got such a tremendous response that eight to twelve people would audition for each role," recalls Keith Martin of his days at Theâtre Charlotte. In response, Martin created The Reading Stage to serve both education and outreach.

"It was a way for an actor to improve three basic skills: script analysis, character development, and oral interpretation. The program focused on the process, not the product."

Promising actors not cast in the mainstage production were invited to take part in The Reading Stage. In workshops and "sessions"—not rehearsals—they dissected a script to look at it from several angles. This became part of the preparation for a readers theater "informance"—not performance—for an audience of family and friends, along with those Martin describes as "hard-core theater addicts."

With only a dozen general rules and two weeks' preparation time, The Reading Stage actors gained insight into their craft and The Reading Stage directors found a whole new way to apply their skills. Under complete staging, a director is unlikely to face three actors playing the same role in one performance. The Reading Stage informances offered that challenge, as explained in this Theatre Charlotte description from the period:

> Please note that participation is unlimited. For example, *'Nite, Mother* contains only two female roles. Yet, twenty-seven men and women analyzed the play, discussed the characters, and orally interpreted the script. The Reading Stage stresses the process rather than the procedure.

Experienced, knowledgeable directors were given complete freedom in assigning lines to the readers; they also may have incorporated choral reading. For one three-act play, the director chose a different cast for each act. For *The Belle of Amherst*, the director used different readers, including some men, for each story. Actors were not the only ones who benefited, however.

"This was a way to audition guest directors," says Martin. "It was like a farm system. We got to see how they work before asking them to direct a mainstage show. Also, directors from other companies came to see the way other directors work. And sometimes the playwright was available to direct the reading."

For the actors, this was not a glamorous gig; it was work. Each session lasted about three hours and centered around an assignment from the previous session. There is a lot of homework, and research at the local library is likely. The informance allowed no costumes, props, blocking, sound effects, nor lighting beyond that needed for illumination. There was no place to hide. It was the simplest equation: words + actors = theater.

Martin says the theater usually had about two dozen participants for each script. "There were nonactors who wanted to broaden their understanding of the acting process. There were techies fascinated by the way actors work. There were people who had no intention of being chosen; they came to audit and then were cast for the informance."

Martin told of a "wonderful by-product" not anticipated when

The Reading Stage was begun: a return of established players. "We got a tremendous turnout of senior adult actors. These people had years of onstage experience, but had not auditioned for some time. We asked them why they came back. Many told us they felt they could no longer carry the burden of memorizing a script. The Reading Stage allowed them to regain their confidence. We cast one woman who never looked at her script during the entire informance. And she thought she was having trouble recalling lines!"

Martin points out that The Reading Stage was a "zero-cost" program. There was no admission charge for the six informances Theatre Charlotte presented each season. Each participant paid $6.50 for a script. Samuel French, among others, offered the rights free for classroom use.

One final benefit: Theatre Charlotte was able to do plays that were not appropriate for its mainstage or for which the rights were not yet available.

"We need new works to reforest the theater," Martin explains, which neatly describes not only the production of new plays, but also the training and development of actors and directors through The Reading Stage program.

Martin still marvels at the number of actors developed and how the acting pool as a whole was greatly increased—thereby giving casting directors a wonderful problem. . . .

29 | *Directors: Did You Know?*

*T*his chapter is a potpourri of tidbits, ideas, perspectives, and resources about auditions, from the director's side of the stage.

Is Your Casting Policy Clear?

It is not uncommon in theater to have questions raised on how shows are cast. Of course, casting is a subjective process, and the decision is usually up to the director. However, if casting is seen as *too* subjective, actors may assume that hidden agendas, prejudices, or favoritism is at work. Here's a simple policy statement given out at auditions by the Topeka Civic Theatre:

> It is the policy of Topeka Civic Theatre to cast regardless of race, color, or disability. Determined by the quality of the auditions, the director will cast the best choice for each role after everyone has had an opportunity to audition. If invited to audition by a director, this does not guarantee that you will be cast. TCT does not precast roles unless announced on the audition notice. In

addition, on occasion, a cast might be expanded to accommodate a large turnout of performers.

Such a policy should be short enough to be readable, but long enough to summarize all the ways your company casts actors in a production. For example, you might want to add to the previous statement: "If after auditions, the director believes that a particular role cannot be cast satisfactorily, other actors may be contacted for a second audition."

While many companies assume that "everybody" knows how auditions and casting work, the truth is that many people don't. To avoid misunderstandings, a simple casting policy is a good idea.

Getting Acquainted

Often a call for auditions fails to pull in enough people because many would-be actors are unfamiliar with the play in question. The Chippewa Valley Theatre Guild of Eau Claire, Wisconsin, came up with a solution that is both fun and effective. All those interested in auditioning for the upcoming play are invited to a play reading. Descriptions of characters are provided, as well as the rehearsal schedule. "Remember, this is not an audition, nor will the director be present for the reading," reads the company's announcement, making a very good selling point. "It is simply an opportunity to become familiar with the script." The reading also is open to those interested in working backstage or in other areas.

Get an Earful

When auditioning actors, director Ted Strickland of the Chattanooga Little Theatre listens carefully. "You may find speech patterns that are unusual and could be used in some way to add variety to your production," he suggests.

Step by Step

Choreographing a musical calls for patience, understanding, and a strong ability to communicate. Motivating performers to do their best is essential, choreographers say. A key in this process is the choreographer's clearly stated role within the production team. "If the cast sees the staff as a team," says choreographer Nancy Santamaria, "respectful of each other's creativity and position, the cast takes their cue and a working attitude of creativity and respect is developed. This structure can really bring a cast together, and even the most in-experienced actor can learn, grow, create, perform, and enjoy the process of theatrical production." The place to begin this teamwork is at the beginning, choreographer Susan Wershing points out: "The choreographer should have a vote in the audition process so those chosen can handle at least the basics. In singing, you can give some-one a lower note, or mask their inadequacy in some other way. But a bad dancer sticks out like the proverbial sore thumb."

The More the Merrier

Encourage company members to attend auditions, whether they in-tend to try out or not. Members can greet newcomers, help them fill out audition sheets, and introduce them to others. They can cheer on those who audition. Their very presence boosts morale and projects an image of a company that really cares about its people. Announce in your company newsletter that nonauditioning members are in-vited, with no pressure on anyone to try out. Then call a few people to act as official hosts.

Keeping Track

It is a good idea to keep a database of all performing members—past, present, and potential. The San Francisco Shakespeare Festival, for example, collects vital information about each actor who auditions and enters it into a computerized database. To call people back for a second audition, the festival sends a personalized letter that tells which role and scenes to rehearse and gives the audition date, time, and location. Then the director gets a report showing audition times and scenes for each character and names of those trying out. As a re-sult, actors and actresses feel good about the festival because of the personal attention they receive. Even if they are not called back, the company sends a personalized letter thanking them for trying out, and asking them to audition again next time.

Let Them Know

Post information about the production at the entrance to the building or room where the auditions are scheduled. Try to anticipate what actors would want to know about your show, including the rehearsal schedule, performance schedule, what parts are being auditioned, and what pages of the script auditioners will be asked to read. Posting this information will save having to repeat it verbally throughout the audition period.

A Friendly Reminder

You may know the frustration of discovering that someone has used your last copy of something—an audition form, for example—so you have to re-create it. To avoid this in the future, put a sticky note on your next-to-last copy, reminding whomever takes it that you need to make more copies.

Through the Years

Actors often don't like telling their ages. The reason is not always vanity—rather, they fear they will be typecast for certain-aged roles. Instead of asking for ages on an audition sheet, consider a multiple choice: "child," "teen," "young adult," or "mature."

Final Words

For directors and actors, there is no absolutely fool-proof guide to a successful audition. We can only point you in the right direction, help you down that road. Success, ultimately, can be measured by only one thing: wonderful acting in a wonderful show. Let us know if you have some additional thoughts on how best to achieve that goal.

Contributors

JILL CHARLES is artistic director of the Dorset Theatre Festival in Dorset, Vermont, an Equity company she cofounded in 1976. She is also the editor/publisher of *Theatre Directories* and a freelance writer for many theater publications.

DIANE CREWS is artistic director of Dreamwrights Youth and Family Theatre in York, Pennsylvania.

LANI HARRIS is an Assistant Professor of Theatre at the University of Central Florida, specializing in acting, directing, and theater careers. She has acted and directed professionally in Los Angeles on stage and in film and video.

NEAL LEWING, with his wife Karen, is owner and director of the Port Polson Players, in Polson, Montana, and artistic director of the Old Prison Players in Deer Lodge, Montana.

LEE MORGAN was operations manager of The Little Theatre, in Winston-Salem, North Carolina.

NANCIANNE PFISTER is associate editor of *Stage Directions*.

DAVID POGUE is a Broadway show conductor as well as a Macintosh trainer and a magic instructor.

GERALD LEE RATLIFF is chair of English/Communications at SUNY-Potsdam in New York state. He is also the author of numerous textbooks on performance and production.

JEAN SCHIFFMAN is a freelance writer in San Francisco, with years of experience with regional auditions. She was cofounder of a midsized theater in San Francisco and is an actor herself.

DAVID SPENCER is a faculty member of the Lehman Engel-BMI Musical Theatre Workshop. He has written lyrics and libretto for *Weird Romance*, the Public Theatre *La Boheme*, and *The Apprenticeship of Duddy Kravitz*.

MORE BOOKS
from Heinemann's *Stage Directions* series

Stage Directions **Guide to Publicity**
Edited by **Stephen Peithman** and **Neil Offen**

The key to getting people into your theatre is getting the word out about it. But if your theatre isn't on Broadway and doesn't have an expensive press agent (or an extensive ad budget), how does it get attention? This book has the answers, including information on what draws an audience to a show, how to improve your mailing pieces, tips for more effective ads, and many other aspects of the publicity game.

0-325-00082-4 / 144pp / 1998

Stage Directions **Guide to Directing**
Edited by **Stephen Peithman** and **Neil Offen**

Every director—from the beginner to the most experienced—will find in this book invaluable information to make their direction more effective. Topics covered include things to look for in an audition, selecting the right play, criticizing effectively, basics of directing a musical, staging a big show with a small cast, blocking tips, managing rehearsals and schedules, and much more!

0-325-00112-X / 144pp est. / Available May 1999

Stage Directions **Guide to Getting and Keeping Your Audience**
Edited by **Stephen Peithman** and **Neil Offen**

Today, theatre competes with many forms of entertainment for people's leisure time. So how does a theatre attract and maintain the audience it needs? You'll find out how in this book, discovering practical suggestions on advertising to motivate ticket-buyers, creating attention-getting mailings, using newsletters, numerous successful marketing and promotion tips, why audiences don't come, and much more!

0-325-00113-8 / 144pp est. / Available June 1999

For more information about these books,
visit us on-line at **www.heinemann.com**,
call 800-793-2154, fax 800-847-0938,
or write: Heinemann, Promotions Dept., 361 Hanover St., Portsmouth, NH 03801.